Garden First In Land Development...

William Webb

Nabu Public Domain Reprints:

You are holding a reproduction of an original work published before 1923 that is in the public domain in the United States of America, and possibly other countries. You may freely copy and distribute this work as no entity (individual or corporate) has a copyright on the body of the work. This book may contain prior copyright references, and library stamps (as most of these works were scanned from library copies). These have been scanned and retained as part of the historical artifact.

This book may have occasional imperfections such as missing or blurred pages, poor pictures, errant marks, etc. that were either part of the original artifact, or were introduced by the scanning process. We believe this work is culturally important, and despite the imperfections, have elected to bring it back into print as part of our continuing commitment to the preservation of printed works worldwide. We appreciate your understanding of the imperfections in the preservation process, and hope you enjoy this valuable book.

GARDEN FIRST
IN
LAND DEVELOPMENT

GARDEN FIRST
IN
LAND DEVELOPMENT

BY

WILLIAM WEBB, F.S.I.

WITH 25 COLLOTYPE PLATES FROM PHOTOGRAPHS

LONGMANS, GREEN AND CO.
39 PATERNOSTER ROW, LONDON
FOURTH AVENUE & 30TH STREET, NEW YORK
BOMBAY, CALCUTTA, AND MADRAS
1919

All rights reserved

GARDEN FIRST
IN
LAND DEVELOPMENT

BY
WILLIAM WEBB, F.S.I.

WITH 25 COLLOTYPE PLATES FROM PHOTOGRAPHS

LONGMANS, GREEN AND CO.
39 PATERNOSTER ROW, LONDON
FOURTH AVENUE & 30TH STREET, NEW YORK
BOMBAY, CALCUTTA, AND MADRAS
1919

All rights reserved

THIS SHORT DESCRIPTION OF A LONG WORK
IS GRATEFULLY DEDICATED TO

SIR ARTHUR SPURGEON, J.P., C.C.

WHO HELPED SO MUCH TO OBTAIN LOCAL GOVERNMENT
FOR THE GARDEN FIRST DISTRICT

PREFACE

In the dark night of the Great War the black sky has been brightened here and there by stars of satisfaction and guidance, and one of these stars—so brilliant that no one could fail to notice it—is the advantage that the civilian has derived from a military training. This education, embarked on through patriotism and accomplished by means of drill, gymnastics and comradeship, would never have succeeded completely had not the citizen who lived much indoors been transferred to an outdoor life in better air.

In this year 1916[1] we assess manhood mainly at its battle value; but when the day of peace dawns, unless our eyes are so dazzled by the sun of prosperity as not to recognise the stars whose help we now freely acknowledge, we shall cultivate manhood for its own sake, and getting back to the land and more healthful conditions will not be lost sight of. Mr. E. Howard's dream of garden cities, pub-

[1] Owing to war conditions the publication of 'Garden First' was postponed until 1919.

lished in 1898 and since given concrete expression at Letchworth, contains the germ of immense national benefits; and, so long as the existing centralism of manufacture and commerce continues, a modified gain may be obtained by providing houses with large gardens apart from the smoke and tainted air of a trade centre.

Land questions are prejudiced by the fact that those who are interested in them are usually divided into two distinct classes, the practical and the theoretical, the former occupied and more or less satisfied with the work in hand, and the latter handicapped for want of personal experience and by inability to realise either the difficulties of carrying their plans into execution or the consequences of so doing. In venturing to place this book before the public, one is encouraged to do so because the theories it puts forth have been proved to a certain extent by the almost completed development of a property on lines indicated in the following pages.

Modesty still whispers that the area to be presently referred to as Garden First is not important enough to warrant a call on people's attention in this day of great things; but its very smallness favours its adoption as an illustration, for it thus comes within the scope of a greater number who may be disposed to follow the example it affords.

CONTENTS

CHAP.		PAGE
I.	Meaning and Objects	1
II.	Hedges and Trees	15
III.	Gardens	39
IV.	Roads	59
V.	Roadside Decoration	67
VI.	Houses	85
VII.	Finance and Law	93
VIII.	The Village	118

ILLUSTRATIONS

NOTE :—The photographs for the illustrations were all obtained on the Garden First Estate since 1915 by the author, who designed the buildings portrayed, except the doorway in Plate VII and the houses that appear in the background of Plates XI and XIII.

FRONT OF A PAIR OF COTTAGES IN THE VILLAGE . . . . . *Frontispiece*

PLATE		FACING P.
I.—a.	TWO-STOREY DETACHED COTTAGE . .	2
	Both the plough and the cottage were within 100 yards of a kerbed and channelled road with houses along its whole length.	
	b. BIG PLOUGH	2
II.—a.	IRON GATES (UNFINISHED) AT THE ENTRANCE TO THE HERBACEOUS AND FLOWERING TREE ROADS	5
	b. A WAR-TIME LAWN. THE LORD MAYOR'S CARRIAGE	5
	He came to the Garden First neighbourhood to open a boys' rifle range on the day the news was received of Lord Kitchener's death, hence the private carriage instead of the state coach.	
III.—a.	MAKING FAST A LOAD OF HAY . . .	7
	Houses are built along the whole length of the other side of the belt of trees to the left.	
	b. DAISY	7
IV.—a.	AN INEXPENSIVE DESIGN FOR A PAIR OF COTTAGES	11
	They depend entirely on Garden First treatment for any good looks they possess.	
	b. FIRM FRIENDS	11
V.—a.	BACK OF ONE OF THE VILLAGE COTTAGES .	17
	b. COTTAGE FLANK WALL	17

ILLUSTRATIONS

PLATE		FACING P.
VI.—a.	The Smithy	25
b.	One of the Topiary Nurseries	25
VII.—a.	Cutting a Hedge to a Point at the Top	27
b.	Doorway of a House built less than Two and a Half Years before the Photo was Taken	27

It was removed from a seventeenth-century house in Sussex, and the climbers are purple clematis and wistaria.

VIII.—a.	A Pair of Cottages in the Village	32
b.	Back Elevation of a Village Cottage	32
IX.—a.	House Roofed with Stone	40
b.	Lily Pool in the Garden of the Lodge at the Entrance to the Rose Road	40
X.—a.	A Poor Crop of Grass	46
b.	A Good Crop of Fruit	46
XI.—a.	The Herbaceous Road seen from the Lodge Garden	53
b.	Conrad F. Meyer in Bloom in May	53
XII.—a.	Entrance Gates to the Bulb Road	59
b.	A Section of the Bulb Road	59
XIII.—a.	Entrance Gates to the Rose Road	67
b.	Exit Gates from the Rose Road	67

The road gates are usually kept open, but were shut to obtain the photos.

XIV.—a.	Lodge at Entrance to Bulb Road	74
b.	Lodge at Entrance to Rose Road	74
XV.—a.	Section of Bulb Border	76
b.	Cottage with Chimney Corner in the Living Room	76
XVI.—a.	A Pair of Typical Garden First Houses	85
b.	Back View of the Same Houses	85
XVII.—a.	Lodge at the End of the Rose Road	90
b.	A Coachman's Cottage	90

ILLUSTRATIONS

PLATE		FACING P.
XVIII.—a.	The Agent to the Garden First Estate	100
b.	The Outside of a Cottage Chimney Corner	100
XIX.—a.	The House where 'Garden First' was written	114
b.	Guernsey Heifers	114
XX.—a.	Lodge at the Entrance to the Herbaceous Road	117
b.	Waiting at the Forge	117
XXI.—a.	The Village Inn, named after the Author's Hero	118
b.	Village Stocks and Whipping Post	118
XXII.—a.	Fire Irons wrought at the Village Smithy	119
b.	Home-made Oak and Iron Harrow	119
XXIII.—a.	The 'Big House' at the Village	120
b.	Sea-Saw on the Green	120
XXIV.—a.	Two Cottages in the Village. In one of these Mr. Hugh Edwards, M.P., has been writing his 'Life of David Lloyd George.'	123
b.	The Village Pond	123

GARDEN FIRST IN LAND DEVELOPMENT

CHAPTER I

MEANING AND OBJECTS

Of the various housing problems, which are in abeyance at the present time, the two most urgent are where the population is on the one hand most scattered and on the other most crowded; and better accommodation for farm labourers and for those at the bottom of city social life is so much needed that it must, before long, have the help of further legislation. It is said that there are nearly a million people in London who live a one-roomed existence, and Mr. Bernard Holland, Chairman of the L.C.C. Housing Committee, wrote on May 2, 1916, to *The Times*: 'The pressure for accommodation among the poorest class is now so severe that it is better they should have bad houses than none at all.'

There are other housing questions of less national importance, and that must be left largely to private enterprise for their solution; and the one that the reader is now invited to consider is neither urban nor rural, nor does the word suburban quite cover its scope, which lies rather between the suburban and the completely rustic. The time when City merchants lived at, or close to, their business belongs to one hundred years ago or more, and the era of suburbs within a horse 'bus ride of St. Paul's pertains to a past generation. A few City men live at the West End, but by far the greater number seek to spend their leisure time and bring up their families at the nearest spot to their work where they can find a comparatively country home; and, the more countrified such a district can be kept, the better it fulfils their requirements. At the same time they do not want the drawbacks incidental to an out-of-the-way countryside, and the object of this book is to explain a system of land development which, while embracing the convenience and luxury of present-day civilization, retains some of those elements of rural life that constitute its attraction.

Those who work their brains at full speed during business hours require more than the rest that is obtained from sleep at night; their minds and nerves require the refreshment that is derived from beautiful surroundings, and from sights, sounds and scents which by their nature and from asso-

PLATE I

ciation are restful. They are the men who will have to pay a large share of the cost of the Great War, and it is mainly they to whom we must look for success in our future trade competition with the Teuton in the East and our more than ever wealthy cousins in the West; and these are reasons, if no other, why this particular branch of housing merits public consideration. It may be said that a prosperous business or professional man is quite capable of making his own home, without outside interference. That is true, as far as the building of his own residence is concerned; but we are not discussing the erection of individual houses so much as the laying-out of estates to meet the needs of those who wish to build for their own occupation.

Many districts must now be contemplating town-planning schemes in order to start work for 'the boys' when they come home. Opinions differ widely as to the probable condition of the labour market after peace is made, but Mr. W. M. Hughes, speaking at the Mansion House on June 21, 1916, said, with reference to the millions of our men now engaged in the war, and the necessity for finding them work afterwards, 'What a tremendous problem! How complex, how difficult! Yet at all hazards we must find a solution or face a situation not less disastrous than the war itself.' The Mayor of a large borough recently stated that his Council were only waiting for peace to begin a relief road; and referring to the horticultural roads on the Garden First Estate as the only ones of their kind in the country, he expressed his desire to make of this new road a rose avenue 1½ miles long on the lines of the one described in Chapter V.

A main reason, however, for publishing at the present time the details of any special class of land development is the considerable amount of town planning which, one imagines, will take place on the Continent when the fighting is over. While many features in the ruined districts will no doubt be reinstated as like the originals as possible, it seems probable that there will be parts where building schemes on new lines will be undertaken. If, in such new construction, any one of the Garden First ideas to be here set forth is thought worthy of adoption in those countries with whom we are now allied in war, this little book will have justified its publication. Horticulture enters largely into Garden First methods, and, surely, in blotting out or at any rate covering up the ghastly past, flowers may find a welcome place.

The area of about 260 acres, the work on which is to be described as offering a small contribution to the subject of land development, is well within

PLATE II

sound of Woolwich guns; and you may tell the time of day by Westminster clock-tower from some of the gardens with the aid of a good glass in clear weather. Moreover, the little snapshot of the Lord Mayor's carriage (Plate II) explains that the locality is within driving distance of the City of London.

One corner of the estate is the scene of much human and mechanical activity. At that angle of the road there are banks and shops, motor-'buses and electric trams, and the whole property, which, when bought, was farm land surrounded on all sides by arable or pasture, is now enclosed by buildings or ground in process of building development. For all this the place is comparatively quiet to the ear and restful to the eye; conditions not easy to prove to those unacquainted with the neighbourhood, but the illustrations may be helpful, and it will emphasise the country tone that prevails to relate how much wild birds and shy beasts still haunt the spot, though there are now 280 houses, or an average of more than one house to an acre.

Hares, rabbits, partridges and wild pheasants have hitherto bred every season notwithstanding their canine and feline enemies. The jay's harsh note by day and the owl's scream by night are common sounds, and sparrow-hawks and kestrels are here unmolested, for 'keepering' is a thing of the past.

Woodcock pay an occasional visit, and this winter one was flushed twice, with an interval of a week, showing he was not discontented with his surroundings. A fox has been reported rarely, though about three years ago one harboured on the estate for some months. Stoats and weasels still have their share of good things, and hedgehogs are often found. Small birds of many kinds there are at their proper seasons—bullfinches, goldfinches, chaffinches, greenfinches, woodpeckers, fly-catchers, butcher-birds, bottle and other tits, wrens, goldcrests, chiff-chaffs, wagtails, whitethroats, linnets in large numbers, lesser red-poles, and larks; and the blackbird exceeds the thrush—a few weeks ago there were twelve blackbirds on a small lawn at one time, and very beautiful they looked. The haw-finch has been an occasional visitor, and doves flit joyously about on summer days. The cuckoo, with his mate, turns up regularly each April, and the hurried whistle of his faithless and undomesticated wife is heard a few weeks later. Wood-pigeons are always plentiful—there were 104 a few days ago all grazing together near the house where this is being written—but their presence is no proof of rusticity, as they are to be found in London; though the fat, heavy specimen of Regent's Park, with his dull plumage, can hardly be recognised as the same kind of bird as his shy cousin who robs

PLATE III

the farmer. Peewits, golden plovers and wheatears have latterly almost deserted the place; but this is probably due quite as much to the fact that trees and hedges have now much enclosed what was previously open land as to the building of houses.

Perhaps nothing shows the curious mixture of (while these lines are being written a sparrow-hawk has flown low down within fifteen yards of the window) town and country more than the following incident. A pair of partridges nested one spring in the angle of the dining-room window, and oviparous feats were consummated; but unfortunately the house was being redecorated at the time, and one of the painters put his foot in the nest and smashed all the eggs.

Mention has been made of the number of hedgehogs, and on Plate III is the portrait of a cow that is supposed to have been injured through being sucked by one. The hedgehog was found curled up in the cow-shed where 'Daisy' was, and one of her teats showed marks corresponding to his teeth. Pains were taken to save the quarter, but without effect, and the known liking of hedgehogs for milk was sufficient *cui bono?* for the vet. to fasten the crime on the little intruder, who was killed; but the worst of it was that a sentence of capital punishment was also passed on the injured cow.

At the time Daisy was photographed she was in the early stages of beef production, and the feeling of well-being was so strong within her that she was unmindful either of the camera two yards from the nostrils that exhaled her delicious breath, or of the flies that stayed undisturbed on her summer coat. Will the kind reader regret that the flies were not removed from the portrait before it was printed? Surely no. The artist who painted a litter of pigs all feeding without a single trotter in the trough probably lived to regret the omission, whether it was due to his idea of refinement or not. There is a well-known painting where one of the figures, a gigantic cherub, is seen in the act of carrying by the legs a cock-pheasant, which he had presumably shot with his bow and arrow. The picture is so pleasing in other respects that one would be inclined to think the artist had reason to know that cherubs carry winged game differently from the method adopted by human sportsmen; but unfortunately *rigor mortis* must have set in while the pheasant was hung up by its head, as the wings are close to its sides; and one is forced to conclude that the model was procured from the poulterer's, which unreality does not satisfy. And so the flies remain, and it is hoped that they will torment the reader no more than they did Daisy.

For the past week a pair of green woodpeckers

have been unusually friendly, spending much of the day so near to the house that, provided one does not startle them by a sudden appearance at the window, one can watch them for some time. Their ape-like attitudes and weird laughter offer some inducement 'To hold opinion with Pythagoras'—Ah! Mr. Woodpecker, 'The evil that men do lives after them.' The report that Circe spread of your flirtation with Pomona may have been circulated by the former to excuse her share in your downfall, but that red face and jerky manner and spigot-like beak certainly point to a pre-existence in which you were much too fond of tapping casks of wine. The sad part is that Mrs. Woodpecker, whose sombre cheeks suggest that if she did at one time give way to alcoholism it was more through trouble than love of revelry, and who still looks quite pretty in her faded green dress, should continue to attend her bacchanalian husband with so watchful a solicitude.

It is not suggested that a new residential neighbourhood can be made to resemble an old country district so closely as to be mistaken for it; but it is believed that, at the place we are now considering, there exists some element which has much in common with what is essentially rural, notwithstanding the introduction of modern sanitation and the conveniences of twentieth-century life;

and while it is difficult to define what this rustic element is, the natural history notes already given are evidence that in some form or other it is there. This little book is written to show how the advance of the house-builder and the increase of population and human occupation may, instead of injuring Nature, so harness her in the exercise of arboriculture and horticulture that she shall be more prolific and, perhaps, more pleasing than before. For nearly thirty years the author has been working out a system with the foregoing objects progressively in view, and it is to give his personal experience, in striving to that end, that the following details will mainly be directed, and not to the usual routine of land development, on which more authoritative information may be obtained elsewhere.

Land developments by individuals and companies vary from philanthropic endeavour to money-making machines, and Garden First is put forward as one which, given favourable conditions, may be undertaken as a business enterprise but with due regard to the public welfare. No suggestion is intended that the work described is a pattern, and certainly not a finished pattern, for others to imitate in its entirety; in fact, any imitation is always greatly handicapped by its very want of originality. At the same time, it is hoped that the explanations may be of use to others

PLATE IV

in working out their own schemes of land development, where the garden is given the consideration it deserves.

The name Garden First means that the garden shall not only have prominence, but that partial garden construction shall be carried out before any buildings are erected, so that there may be pleasant shade of trees, and the shelter afforded by live hedges and matured shrubs, before houses are built. A distinctive attribute of Garden First development is the arrangement of the entire estate in such a way that the occupiers of houses not only have the enjoyment of their own premises in desirable seclusion, but that, both from their own upper windows and when passing along the roads, it may appear as though they are in one large garden of which their own holding is a part. Thus the individual obtains his share of, and supplies his quota to, the common fund of enjoyment.

Another feature is that the public may enjoy a considerable proportion of the arboriculture and horticulture of the place without infringing seriously the privacy of the residents, to whose maintenance of the flower-borders in a comparatively open position they are indebted for the view. There are instances where this idea of allowing the people to see some of the flowers, or lawn, is carried out by a few residents in most neighbourhoods, and the fact that the main part of the garden is hidden rather adds to than detracts from the pleasure of those passers-by who are not of a dissatisfied nature; for there is much truth in the saying that a garden half concealed is a garden best revealed.

That more men do not study the wayfarer in the construction and maintenance of their pleasure-grounds is certainly due in greater measure to want of thought than want of heart; and a little consideration will show that the aggregate advantages of a semi-public display are sufficiently great to warrant its more frequent adoption. The proprietor's enjoyment of his flowers is heightened by the knowledge that he is giving pleasure to many others, and the joy of the numerous passers-by is increased by the feeling of goodwill which a present always possesses beyond the intrinsic value of the gift. Therefore, if one may use a word which to-day implies a duty, and yesterday represented a vice, and the day before a virtue, one would say that the suggested common ability to enjoy the same horticulture is sound 'economy.'

With regard to the illustrations of houses, it should be pointed out that they have not been introduced for their architectural merit, but rather to show how any simple and restrained style of building may be made more attractive by Garden

First methods; and as an extreme case in point, the following letter by the author to *The Times*, in 1913, may be quoted on the subject of horticulture as a house-decorator:

Rural Housing and Sentiment.

The need for more labourers' cottages is so great that most people are prepared to further their erection even at the risk of some lessening of the beautiful in the countryside. At the same time such an effect would mean a serious ethical and economic loss, and I venture to suggest a simple and practical method of overcoming the difficulty.

In order to build a sanitary cottage of a given size at the lowest possible cost, any deviation from the cheapest method of construction in order to gain architectural effect is out of the question. Even in cases where some slight excess is permitted, the result will often be decreased stability or impaired ventilation in an attempt to follow the garden suburb fashion of the present day.

The remedy consists in the rapid growth of hardy climbers, which, in a short time, are capable of transforming the ugliest cottage into an object of admiration to the passer by. They (the climbing roses, honey-suckle, jessamine, clematis montana, ampelopsis and many others) would also prove a strong home-tie to the tenant, as none of the working classes have a greater unconscious appreciation of the beautiful than the average rustic.

The cost would only be a few shillings per house, but, in order to be successful, the idea would have to be systematically carried out. First by wiring the new walls, and secondly, by the supply of young plants. The latter could be propagated at one or more nurseries established for the purpose and sent by post with a leaflet on planting, watering, &c., and there is little doubt that local horticultural societies could be inspanned to further the project.

At the same time the Garden First Estate has benefited greatly by the work of well-known architects, whose designs would be considered excellent quite apart from a garden setting. And now, having sketched out the general aims and principles governing Garden First development, we may proceed to a more detailed consideration of the practical working of a property on those lines.

CHAPTER II

HEDGES AND TREES

THE first step in evolving the Garden First system was, as from the year 1888, to entirely discard ugly wooden boundary fences. Wood fences are expensive to erect and soon in need of repair, for the sappy oak posts start rotting almost as soon as they are in the ground. The split-pales do not lie close together, and are therefore by no means draught-proof as shelter either for ourselves or for trained fruit-trees or vegetation generally. For crowded districts where there are no gardens to speak of, the wood fence is a necessity. And a low oak ring-fence round a large park in the pure country air soon weathers and becomes host to lichen, and thus quickly adapts itself to its environment: by its encircling length it attains a measure of dignity that a post and pale boundary can never possess along the four sides of an ordinary dwelling. A large estate recently changed hands, and one of the first things the purchaser did was to remove the old silvered oak fence and replace it with a high new one, so constructed that the pales were reversed between each pair of posts, and the whole was then stained brown; by these means its appearance of easy continuous extent was interfered with and the restoring hand of Nature was stayed.

In place of the dead fence it was decided to make live hedges an essential part of Garden First, and the question was, what kind of shrub would be most suitable for the purpose. It must be quick-growing, evergreen, not likely to die off, and well able to bear transplanting even at an advanced age; because it sometimes happens that an alteration must be made in the position of a boundary; or an opening or gateway is required, which necessitates making good between the gate-posts and the remaining portion of the live fence. The shrub decided upon was privet, and after one or two experiments the common variety was chosen. It is the more evergreen kind, and it certainly makes an excellent hedge, which, when well clipped, is similar to box in appearance; but it is not of rapid growth, and is inclined to straggle. A small estate was laid out with these hedges, in some fifty plots, and so strange a proceeding did it then appear to the public that the owner was thought to be almost bereft of his senses. Mrs. Grundy was alarmed—it was really

PLATE V

not quite decent to have a garden without a fence round it. However, one can become accustomed to almost anything, and the hedge has now taken the place of the wood barrier on nearly every building estate in the neighbourhood; you may walk in one direction for some miles through thousands of acres in course of development, and see live fences for plot boundaries all the way.

But to return to the kind of privet that is best for the purpose. The oval-leaf variety (*Ligustrum ovalifolium*) is on the whole quite the best; it is a very rapid and straight grower and can be kept evergreen by cultivation and by the aid of a little manure every few years. Some people are inclined to deprecate the use of this shrub; one will say it is too greedy and robs the adjacent ground of its nourishment, and there is some truth in the statement; but this disadvantage can be overcome by a process to be explained later when we come to the description of an herbaceous border planted right up to a hedge. Another critic will say that privet does not give him the artistic effect he requires, and will propose the use of box, yew, or holly, each of which, no doubt, makes an excellent fence round individual gardens, or, better still, for their internal divisions, but not one of the suggested substitutes combines the advantages which have just been attributed to privet. They grow slowly and, except when quite young, move badly; so that the satisfactory filling up of gaps in a matured hedge would be difficult and costly; and, as there are about twenty miles of live fence on the estate now under consideration, the use of one of the suggested substitutes would have been wellnigh impossible. Yew has the additional drawback of being very poisonous, and to plant it within reach of horses is not fair. The yew-tree is very common in this neighbourhood, and it seems as though animals brought up amongst it are aware of its dangerous quality, but even pheasants, when imported from other parts, have been killed by it.

A welcome change may be made by the insertion of beech here and there in a privet hedge, but the constant practice all over an estate would be more monotonous than the sole use of the latter shrub. Again, *Prunus cerasifera*, which has come much into use of late years, makes a very good hedge. It is quick-growing, difficult to penetrate, its early flowers are welcome though they do not make a great show, and it has a pleasant habit of turning its small twigs green in the latter part of the winter as a foretaste of spring; but it does not retain its foliage throughout the year, the power to do which should be an essential feature of a live fence round a garden.

Before we continue the subject of hedges, one

would like to have a clear understanding on this point, viz. that everything in arboriculture and horticulture must be done well, or it were better to leave it alone. To buy so many thousand leggy young privet and stick them in a row, with the idea that because they are hardy shrubs there will soon be a luxuriant hedge without any more trouble, will probably cause much disappointment. It ought not to be necessary to say this, but when one sometimes sees rose-trees in the last stage of poverty and atrophy, and one hears the grower who supplied them blamed for their want of vitality, which is evidently due to the purchaser's lack of care in planting and cultivation, it seems necessary to make some emphatic statement as to the importance of right methods.

In order then to carry out Garden First methods well, it will probably be necessary to keep one or more nurseries always going, so that there may be a supply of trees and shrubs ready to hand of a larger size and more bushy growth than could be obtained from a distance, without great expense and considerable risk owing to the length of time the things would be out of ground. From the home nursery deciduous trees may be moved after standing there ten or twelve years, and evergreen trees and shrubs eight years, without the fear of losing any or even of giving them a serious check. A sojourn of two or three years in that place, with annual pruning, will produce privet which will make a good hedge at once, and one that will attain any desired height in a very short time. It is not advisable to propagate; in fact it is probably cheaper and certainly saves much time and trouble to buy quite young stock from one of the well-known trade nurseries, for choice one 300 or 400 feet higher than the property to be developed.

If it were decided to lay out the whole of an estate at once it might be well to carry out all the planting immediately, with quite small hedges and trees, as soon as the plans were drawn for the proposed roads and their adjacent building sites; and in this way a nursery would not be necessary, as the young trees would grow up *in situ*. It is probable, however, that it will take something like a quarter of a century to dispose of 200 to 300 acres, and it is almost impossible to decide so long before exactly what sized plots will be required, or, with the uncertainty of what may happen to a neighbourhood, the class of property for which a demand will exist at so remote a period. Again, if a complete scheme of development is decided on in detail from the commencement, there will probably be a greater lack of originality and personality than if the various roads are thought out as the years go by, and further experience of the past forms from time to time a fresh starting-point for some new idea. Garden First work should be practised as an art and not reduced to a science.

The nursery should, therefore, form part, and a very important one, of the operations, and it is by no means the least interesting. Young trees and shrubs thrive so well there, as though they enjoyed and benefited by each other's company, and it is a pleasure to watch their health and rapid growth. In choosing the position of it, nearness to that portion of the estate for which its trees will be required is an important factor, and it should be close to a cart-road.

As to soil, the roots will fibre best in rather light and friable loam, but on the other hand a stiff soil hangs together better when removing with a ball. In good trade nurseries it is the custom to shift trees and shrubs every two years, and this certainly causes them to make an abundance of fibrous roots; but it becomes expensive, and it is not necessary where a home nursery is kept up, because of the ease and celerity with which replanting in permanent positions can be carried out.

It does not matter, as far as light and air are concerned, whether the rows run North and South or East and West, but it is well that the part which is used for the more delicate varieties should be surrounded by a sheltering hedge. Privet two or three deep will answer well for this; and where the screen runs at right angles to the nursery lines, the plants composing it should be put in linear with the rows to enable the horse-hoe to work right through, and plenty of room should be left outside for the horse and hoe to turn. This is important, for the difference in cost between horse and hand labour in all farm work is very considerable, besides which the horse-hoe does the work more thoroughly. The width of the rows and space between trees varies with what kinds are used, but allowance should be made for horse-hoeing during four or five years' growth, so that the young things may have every encouragement through their early stages. After that time the hardier sorts need no further stimulant in the shape of cultivation, and the ground may be roughly sown with rye-grass to keep it tidy. While on the subject of hoeing, a word about harness may not be out of place. Care should be taken that no part of it obtrudes more than is necessary, and that the chains, tugs, and whippen ends are covered over with some soft leather, to be renewed as often as it wears through. A steady, narrow-shaped, neat-footed horse should be chosen, and one not too fond of biting the twigs, or it must be muzzled. The hand-hoe should follow the horse one, and the men must be warned over and over again not to hoe quite close up to the stems, as

HEDGES AND TREES

even a little scratch may grow into a nasty bark-wound, and the hoe should have rounded points to lessen the risk.

If there is any fear of hares or rabbits, it is best to completely enclose the nursery with strong wire-netting 1 foot in the ground and 4 feet out, and the gateways should have hard thresholds. Rabbits are a difficulty, as they have a special liking for the bark of fruit-trees and that of any newly planted ones. In the early stage of development one can shoot them, but when houses multiply it becomes dangerous to do so for fear of ricochetted shots; the irreparable damage the little beggars do to young trees is out of all comparison to the sport they afford, and the number of small ownerships makes it impossible to entirely eradicate them when once they are established. Wiring and trapping are so cruel that one is loath to resort to these methods, and, when shooting becomes impracticable, a few couple of strong beagles answer well, especially if they are helped here and there by long nets such as poachers use. On the outbreak of war the beagles here were destroyed to save their food, but the rapid increase since in the number of rabbits is causing serious inconvenience. A little soot or raw manure round any plants it is specially desired to preserve seems to keep them off, and fruit-trees may be protected in winter by a coating of cow-dung, tar, paraffin, and water. Another scare for rabbits consists of little sticks about 8 inches long fixed upright in the ground with a slit in the top in which is inserted half a sheet of note-paper folded twice to make it stiffer.

Bobs, a clumber spaniel, played such a useful part in Garden First development that it is hoped some little notice of him may be forgiven, as he did much towards lessening the ground-game and to minimise the suffering of the wounded. As a pup he would fetch a hen's egg without cracking it. He never wanted breaking in, as his inherited instincts were so good that he seemed to grow up always doing the right thing with as little fuss and noise as possible. When he knew a rabbit was in a tussock of grass, and it was unwilling to bolt, instead of rushing in at it he would just cock his ears and wag his stump, and then, if bunny did not move, Bobs would hold up his paw and gently tap the grass till the quarry, seeing the dog was in earnest, was forced to take the open. Sometimes after a long hunt for a wounded bird his owner would give it up, and soon after turn round to see the dog quietly walking at his heels with the partridge in its mouth. Nothing ever made Bobs angry, and he would pull along a winged old cock-pheasant by the neck so gently as not to hurt a feather, for all the kicks and scratches he received. Like most clumbers,

PLATE VI

inbreeding told somewhat on the vigour of his constitution, and deafness and infirmity made his end advisable at about his eighth year.

And now to avoid being accused of anecdotage we must return to the practical details of forestry in miniature. The kinds of trees to be bought will vary according to the soil they are expected to grow in, but still more with regard to the quality of decoration fitted to the scheme of development decided on—whether a rough-and-ready effect is desired, by the use of very hardy sorts that give a good show without much trouble, or whether specimens more delicate and requiring greater care are sought, in order to appeal to the expert horticulturist.

Experience teaches that it is more useful not to plant very largely at one time, and about 30,000 trees and shrubs (besides privet) will probably be enough to start with for an estate of 250 acres, and then every few years another nursery can be made with, say, another 15,000 or 20,000. Fondness of the work has been responsible for much overplanting here; one nursery contained about 150,000, including privet, and at the beginning of this season there were 500 cut box-trees in various nurseries, where they had been trimmed for the past twelve years, as opportunities for the use of topiary work are infrequent. The number of privet required can be easily worked out, because a hedge takes two rows, each with plants on an average 1 foot 3 inches apart. With the more expensive varieties it pays to buy, in addition to what will be required in the early stages of development, a number of very young trees and shrubs, as they are much cheaper than larger specimens, and they cost no more per head to maintain than the commoner sorts, while their yearly increase in value is much greater.

One of the difficulties to contend with is that if small trees are planted in the nursery at an ordinary distance apart they soon become so crowded that they require thinning out before the removes are ready to set out permanently. One excellent way of overcoming this is to plant the trees about 8 feet from one another, and to fill in between with privet, which will be ready for removal for hedges as soon as the trees require more space, and in the meantime its shelter is very welcome to the little saplings. It is important to deep-plough and well cultivate the ground before planting; and, if it is weedy, a summer fallow is advisable. Whether any manure is required depends on the soil, but it is better not to give a heavy dressing, or the trees will go back on being planted out. If any variety does not make satisfactory progress it is easy to give a top-dressing, and this is best done in October, for the effect of it in that month, especially on evergreens, is extraordinary.

PLATE VII

If it is intended to have permanent woodland of any size it is well, if possible, to fix the site of a nursery on that spot, and then the wood can be formed by leaving trees at right distances apart where they are growing. In any case a few trees or shrubs may be left here and there as specimens.

In forming hedges it is advisable to run some wire-netting between the two rows of privet to make a more effectual barrier; for the wire and the hedge together are a much more formidable obstacle to clamber than either would be without the other. It is unnecessary to have any strainers, and some little wooden stakes are sufficient to keep the netting in its place till it is retained there by the growth of the hedge. It is undesirable to make a wire-netting boundary fence with a hedge on one side of it, as the wire interferes with the free growth of the adjoining privet.

There are various fashions for cutting hedges. That curving to a point at the top is good, and looks exceedingly well when done properly, but it requires an expert with a fagging hook and shears; and, when sections of one hedge are in different ownership, the respective gardeners are less likely to produce a uniform effect than if the hedge is cut square at the top. The sides of a hedge should be cut upwards with a hook and not trimmed with shears, as the latter plan is harder work and takes longer.

In moving privet from the nursery to the site of a new fence, there will be no difficulty in lifting with a good ball, but the men must be cautioned against knocking any of the earth off, either purposely, or by inadvertently jarring the plants on unloading. Privet produces a great quantity of fibre, except in clay, and if the ball of earth is shaken off, it is better to cut off some of the fibre than to plant it as a flattened mat. Privet hedges, unlike quick, do much better at the bottom of a bank than the top; and if two were planted at the same time on those different levels, that at the bottom would soon reach a greater height than the top of the one above it. These hedges should not be allowed to flower, which condition is both the cause and effect of poor growth. It is usual to tread in trees and shrubs well when planting, but the practice here is only to harden the earth sufficiently to uphold the things planted, and the rain soon consolidates the mould without the risk of its becoming caked. An exception should be made to this rule when dealing with very light soils or roses.

And now with regard to tree planting. It has been the custom on the Garden First Estate to set out two or more rows of trees and shrubs on each side of a party hedge; the larger deciduous trees nearest the fence, pines and firs next, and shrubs and flowering trees on the outer sides of the belt.

Where the plot is an acre or more, the side belts widen out into a round clump of trees and shrubs immediately behind the building line, to provide a more complete screen between the houses which it is hoped will come later.

A good deal of preparation is required to render the ground fit to receive the new plantation. Speaking from experience of a chalk subsoil, it is much better to cultivate the whole surface than to dig a hole for each tree. First the land is ploughed and fallowed till the turf fibre is nearly rotten, then it is well harrowed, and next the large plough described in the chapter on Roadside Decoration is used to go right down to the chalk. This treatment provides the greatest obtainable amount of cultivated soil, and leaves the bottom a hard, smooth surface, which there is no temptation for the roots to penetrate, and so they all spend their time profitably in obtaining as much nourishment as possible.

One of the most difficult points to decide is the distance which shall be kept from row to row and from tree to tree. If planted near together they soon become crowded, and if kept farther apart no screen is provided for the first few years. Perhaps the better plan is to plant near together, and thin out a few years hence; but somehow or other the thinning-out time never comes, as one dislikes the gaps which it necessitates. The need of a drastic thinning out on this estate has been brought home by the difficulty that has been experienced in obtaining photographs of whole houses.

Another vexed question is that of staking. Unless trees of fair size are moved with a very heavy ball, they need some support for at least the first year after transplanting; and experience proves that however carefully a tree is staked, the constant rocking to and fro in the wind sooner or later disarranges the protecting material, which has been supplied to keep the top and side of the stake from rubbing against the bark, and a nasty wound is made that will always be a disfigurement. After experimenting for some years with stakes, they have been entirely abandoned here in favour of wiring. A small piece of old cloth or sacking is tied round the trunk about 5 feet from the ground with some tarred cord. Next, three stout stakes, about 3 feet long, and technically known as bats, are driven well into the ground about 4 feet away from the tree, slightly in the direction of the latter, and forming the corners of an equilateral triangle. Wires are then fastened round the tree outside the sacking and attached also to the three stakes. By this plan the tree is held firmly in its place without any risk of injury to the bark, and the only

HEDGES AND TREES

thing to remember is to remove the wire and tarred cord before they cut into the trunk by reason of its rapid growth. This method is particularly adapted for large trees, and its only drawbacks are that the wires are apt to trip people up and that they must be temporarily removed each time the horse-hoe is used.

In transplanting trees from the nursery to the place they are intended to occupy permanently, a tool called a graft, which is a long, narrow spade, is used. The practice adopted in these nurseries is to dig round the specimen to be lifted a trench rather more than 1 foot deep and about 12 inches from the trunk of trees of moderate size. All roots that protrude into the trench are cut through, and then the men employed drive their grafts underneath the ball level with the bottom of the trench, and the tree is ready to be lifted. The roots which have been roughly severed during this operation are now cut off with seccateurs, as a knife tends to loosen the earth in the ball. A knife should never be used to cut a tree-root unless the latter is firmly fixed or held; it does not require much outward strain to split a root away from the trunk or larger root from which it springs, and the length of the root that is cut provides leverage. The ball is now tied up in a piece of sacking or old canvas and carted to be planted *in situ* after removing the covering. In taking up trees without much fibre from a very light soil it is a good plan to tie up the ball first in a piece of old fish-netting, and then to use the canvas as an outer wrap: on arriving at the position to be occupied by the tree the canvas is removed, but not the net, which is planted with the ball.

When it is required to move quite large trees and shrubs, or even moderate sized ones out of season, the following plan has been found to work satisfactorily. A square yard is marked out, with the tree in the centre, and a trench is dug round the four 3-feet sides, keeping the latter perpendicular. The block of earth is then boxed in by nailing stout boards round it to the depth of 2 feet 6 inches, after which the men proceed to undermine it immediately beneath two opposite sides of the box. When it has been undercut from 6 inches to 9 inches, boards are nailed on to the underneath edge of the wooden sides and wedged up by bricks or stone. This operation is repeated till the big lump of earth is enclosed, and the tree may be transplanted in the middle of summer without a leaf fading. The whole thing is then loaded on to a cart or van by rollers on stout planks; it is rather risky work in wet weather, but the foreman here is a very capable man, and there has never been a mishap so far.

Most deciduous trees require siding up once and again in their early days, that is to say the lower

PLATE VIII

HEDGES AND TREES

branches are cut off in order to make a tall and shapely specimen. If this operation is long delayed it not only makes more work, but the marks of the operation are never quite obliterated by the growth of the bark, notwithstanding its considerable ability in that direction; the cut should be clean with a sharp knife close to the stem. After siding up trees or thinning out a plantation, young shoots will start from the main trunks, and these should be rubbed off with the hand directly they appear.

Unless the summer which follows the season in which a new plantation has been made is an exceptionally wet one, the trees will require watering during any dry periods that occur. If the site to be watered happens to be near a main, the simplest way is to rent meters from the Company, and attach a hose to the supply pipes, which will have been laid on to plots facing the new road; the only drawback to this method being the coldness of the water. When no main happens to be near the trees, the work must be done by a water-cart or van, and the supply can be drawn from the nearest fire hydrant, or what is better, from a large open tank into which the water has previously flowed through a hose or small supply pipe. If the tank is large and always kept refilled, one obtains a supply of soft water of a like temperature to the air.

The following suggestion—made without personal experience—may possibly be useful. It is that on starting an important land development it would be profitable to sink an artesian well, which would provide water for trees and estate work generally, and also for the use of builders erecting houses on the land, as a water-company's charge for the latter is sometimes out of all proportion to the rates at which they are bound to furnish a supply by meter for other purposes.

A few hours after trees—or for that matter any other kinds of vegetation—have been watered, it is necessary to scratch over the surface of the ground to prevent it caking. If this is neglected, cracks will appear in the soil, and they will act as drains to carry off all the moisture, so as a general rule, it is better not to water at all than to do so without returning to disintegrate the surface of the ground. When beds were constructed along the rose road described in Chapter V, careful arrangements were made for summer watering, and three iron tanks, containing over 1,000 gallons each, were purchased in which to soften water; but it was discovered that all through a long dry spell no artificial watering was necessary, or even desirable, as the constant use of the Sproughton hoe kept the prepared soil sufficiently moist. Tanks used for storing water should be placed high enough to allow a cart to remain at such a level as will permit the whole of the water to be drawn off, and the simplest form of stand on which to perch the miniature reservoir is a mound of earth, the sides of which can be sown with grass. When a very large tank is required it is better made of concrete, 1 foot thick and rendered on the face. Whenever concrete is used for holding water it is advisable to reinforce it with a little iron or stout wire to prevent the risk of a fracture.

For the first two years after a belt of trees has been planted the ground should be cultivated by the horse- and hand-hoes, and at the expiration of that time it may be sown with grass-seed to save future labour. The grass will require cutting twice a year, and this is best done with a fagging hook—if a scythe is used the snead is certain to bark the trees. Each autumn the leaves should be raked or swept up to prevent them rotting the grass, and for the further reason that they are very useful as bedding for cattle and subsequent top-dressing for the fields.

Without going deeply into the subject of insect pests, there are three kinds which have been so troublesome here that a short reference to them may not be out of place. One is the spruce gall *aphis*, which makes little things like cones on the small branches of young spruce, and which, if not kept in check, is likely to ruin the appearance of the tree and seriously injure its vitality. It may be discovered about the end of April in the shape of little spots of a white woolly substance on the under side of the branches, and if not dealt with at that stage the galls must be picked off by hand and burnt as soon as they are seen. It can be sprayed in the former condition with a paraffin solution, and care must be taken to work the spray up underneath the branches. Before we leave the spruce, a word of warning may be given as to its liability to injury through being whipped by other trees, such as birch, if they are near enough to rub against it in windy weather.

Another troublesome pest is the grub of the pine bud-moth, and its presence may be detected in Scotch fir by a broken-down appearance of the young leader as soon as the latter is about 3 or 4 inches long. On closer examination it will be noticed that some resin has been discharged where the young shoot left the last year's growth, and if the deformed twig is touched it easily comes off. A little hole may then be discovered in the centre of it, and about $\frac{1}{2}$ inch up is found the grub that caused the damage. If the whole of the injured leaders are picked off and burnt a check is given to this very injurious insect. It is said that this pest and the spruce gall *aphis* are only troublesome where large numbers of conifers are planted together without intervening deciduous trees, but that is not the experience on this estate.

Another most harmful insect is the beech *cocus*, which attacks trees of mature growth. It is easily identified by the white mycelium which covers patches of this minute creature on the trunks and branches of beech-trees. A leaflet published gratis by the Board of Agriculture gives the best remedies, and it is wise to take the necessary trouble to destroy this pest, otherwise it will soon kill large branches and eventually the whole of a magnificent tree.

On looking over this chapter it seems very dry reading, but the subject of which it treats is most interesting: the dryness must be due to defective treatment and to the remoteness that at present characterises all pre-war occupations. In the return to more simple life and pleasures, which is expected as one result of the trial we are passing through, tree planting may well take a part. Cicero, the learned Latin, whose treatise on the joys of age was one of the chief sorrows of the present writer's youth, recommended the growing of trees as a hobby for old people, and Caecilius said, 'He plants trees, to benefit the next generation'; but why should not young folk be encouraged to practise arboriculture, so that they may enjoy the fruits of their labour during the rest of a long life? A boy born at

Garden First planted, or to be more accurate, helped to plant, a mulberry-tree on his first birthday, with the result that he is now able to pack a basket of the fruit in his tuck-box after the summer holidays.

CHAPTER III

GARDENS

A GREAT deal has been said and written about the influence of environment and the impossibility of raising the submerged tenth before their housing is improved. Environment does not act automatically, but it cannot be denied that the power of its influence is enormous; and while it is unnecessary to admit the right of the slum-dweller to the first consideration, it does not follow that folk of good social standing do not feel the beneficial effect of being suitably environed; in fact, their habits and training often render their senses fully alive to surrounding influences. The inference is that the application of Garden First principles is of much advantage to a highly strung nature, and the use of a beautiful garden for leisure and contemplation not only tends to lift the mind to high thoughts, but may even bring to the man of affairs a touch of mysticism.

Quiet intercourse with nature sometimes brings

men very near the unseen and the most beautiful, as witness ancient Hebrew poetry, written without the clearer knowledge we possess through more recent sacred history and sacramental evidence; and there is no reason why we, who have inherited the latter aids, should relinquish the former as an antidote to humanism; and if this topic seems too anagogical in a book on land development, the reader will perhaps forgive its inclusion when he recollects the time in which the writing occurred. Let us for a moment take one or two common instances of the consideration of life in its lower forms. Take for example a colony of ants hurrying to and fro and watch them at the time of their pre-nuptial flight. We Occidentals with our ceaseless activity are not so often in need of an impetus to work as the more sluggish Oriental, but we can yet learn our lesson from the tiny insect. The string of inventions during the past 100 years is apt to make mankind feel they can unaided reach perfection; yet the most recent and perhaps most marvellous of human contrivances has only brought us in one respect to the level of the ants, who (with white ants) of all nature are most like airmen, for some of these little creatures have not only the power of flying but also of removing their wings on coming back to earth.

Again, no craft can provide a stronger analogy, in proof of a future and fuller existence, than one

PLATE IX

which constantly shows that the decomposition of the apparently dead seed is necessary to produce fresh and more plentiful life; and so the garden helps to assure one that one's *ego* does not depend for existence on the preservation of one's casing. Until faith in the defeat of death is universally held and acted on, War—that strange mixture of nobility and hell—must, with its preparation, be endemic, but, meantime, we believe of this or that dear one who has given his life for his friends that

> 'What we trust unto the dust
> Is but the earthly garb he wore.'

While there is much to appeal to one's reason by the study of nature in detail, there is also a subtle influence on one's inner self by the involuntary absorption of a certain restfulness that is frequently experienced in a beautiful garden. This delightful sensation is due to a combination of many factors: to colours that are at peace with one another, to the correct placing of trees and shrubs, to paths that express their meaning by being best adapted to their purpose, to straight lines that are really straight, to correct tangential curves, to the graceful form and due proportion of the fittings that are there, to the gentle rise and fall of music in the tree-leaves, to the blending of a dozen unnoticed perfumes into one, to the lazy hum of insects' wings, to clearly apparent skill and care in the maintenance of all the garden in its highest perfection, to the knowledge that so much of what has been done was handwork under the blue dome, and, in fact, to the combined efforts of the artist and the craftsman working directly on and with Nature.

> Paradise Lost was the Garden of Eden,
>   Paradise Gained is the Garden of Sleep,
> Where we shall rest till the great Resurrection
>   Out of the soil or the depths of the deep.
>
> Gardens of earth, with your fragrance and beauty,
>   Sing to my sad heart some joy on the way,
> Wrap me around with the glories of nature,
>   Where for a while would I restfully stay.

It is but rarely we find a garden of the most perfect type, as it seems only to reach its zenith under what are to most of us impossible conditions. It is when the pleasance is flanked on one side by ancient stone or brick, and on the other by park-trees born hundreds of years ago, that one realises the literal meaning of the word 'inspiration' and inhales deep draughts of beauty. Fortunately, however, we do not need always to live at concert pitch, and what we miss in superexcellence of art we make up by love of home, and, so long as the dominant note of æsthetic influence is rest, we may derive infinite enjoyment from our own gardens. But beware of the scarlet geranium for, though he may be quite docile in a cottage window, and harmless in the grassy avenue at Hampton Court, in a garden of roses he will try to bite anyone who comes within reach. The arrogant Viola Bullion is another unprofitably gay offender and, except under special conditions, should be treated on similar lines to those advised by a celebrated physician in dealing with drinking-water of doubtful purity, viz. to filter it and then boil it for ten minutes, then filter again and boil for ten minutes more, and, after filtering and boiling a third time, to throw it away. Viola Bullion is, unfortunately, almost as easy to grow as a dandelion, and for years these plants were put up with in a certain garden in the hope that by reducing their numbers and much snubbing they could be restrained from domineering over all their neighbours; but it was of no avail, and one day in June, after—forgive the hyperbolism—the entire household had suffered from insomnia, and after strong hints from special constables to shade the wretched creatures at night, the whole company went off in a wheel-barrow, 'unwept, unhonoured, and unsung.' There are many gardens where a knowledge of horticulture, generous expenditure and infinite care combine to produce a brilliant effect, but the feeling of rest is conspicuous by its absence, for the scent of the flowers seems to be overpowered by the smell of new paint and varnish.

Work in the garden is a healthy form of exercise for the body and recreation for the mind, and spade-work is said to employ more different muscles than any other occupation. On the borders of France and Spain is a religious house called the Convent of the Silent Sisters, where the inmates subject themselves to penance by abstaining from all speech, except for a quarter of an hour once a year. Noise of all kinds is prevented as far as possible, to which end the floors are covered with a foot of dry sand; moreover, the hoods of the nuns are gathered in round the face till the opening is no larger than the glass of a diving-dress. The punishment is so severe and so prolonged that it would tend to unhinge the reason of the sufferers but for one thing, and that is that their time is largely employed in gardening.

The use of the word 'home' just now recalls the wide difference there is between a cottage garden and an allotment. The latter grows first-rate vegetables, and the bit of ground with its misshapen shed is a great help to a man with no garden of his own. It has, however, the drawback of being at some distance, so that it entails undesirable exercise at the end of a day's work, and often by the time the cabbage-patch is reached the light is gone. Artistically there is, perhaps, no greater trial to a town than the average allotment ground. This is mainly due to the lack of symmetry in the sheds already referred to; and, inasmuch as the allotments are often the first part which is seen as one approaches the town by train—or worse still, is kept waiting outside—it would pay local authorities to provide, at the public expense, well-proportioned structures with span roofs, and so avoid an unfavourable first impression on the visitor.

When a working-man has sufficient land with his cottage the above drawbacks do not exist, and there is the moral advantage, which his wife and family share with him, in having a garden of their own, with the domestic felicity that it usually promotes. On the economic side there is not only the value of the vegetables grown, but the avoidance of spending money to buy enjoyment of a less healthy kind elsewhere. Reference has already been made to the influence of environment, and if every working-man had a proper garden round his cottage, the power for good on this and future generations would indeed be great. Of course, in towns this is impossible, but every legitimate effort should be made to induce those who build cottages in suburban and country districts to allow as much ground as the occupier can easily cultivate; and rating authorities should not hinder this by assessing the land at more than it is worth to the tenant as garden. They would not lose, as in the long run they would gain by the increased prosperity of the neighbourhood. We go away for a month's delightful holiday in the summer, and regret at its expiration is reduced by the recollection of the pleasant garden that awaits our return. But who has come back to, say, Liverpool Street Station, who has not felt a guilty pang as he looked down from the railway carriage on the sordid streets of poorer London. We quiet our consciences to a certain extent by reflecting that if the inhabitants of that drab district do not like it they can in many instances move into the country and obtain work there, but we cannot quite blot out the contrast between their lot and ours. For in cities most enjoyments cost money, and therefore the difference between poverty and wealth is always felt even with good wages. On the other hand, most of the pleasures of the country are free and common to all; we breathe the like fresh air, read the same book of nature, and live similarly an outdoor life; agriculture, gardening and foresting are general interests; and, in as much as these sciences delight us in proportion to our practical knowledge and skill, it follows that the man must often obtain more gratification from their pursuit than the master does. The expert farm labourer loves the work in which his cunning hand excels, and so fixes his personality on what he achieves that his occupation becomes an art.

PLATE X

GARDENS

A large area of ground to each house is an essential feature of Garden First development. The larger the gardens are in proportion to the buildings the more thoroughly the spirit of the scheme is carried out, but it must not be forgotten that the intending resident has to consider the cost of upkeep, as well as the purchase price of the ground. To a certain extent this difficulty may be overcome by planting some portion of each of the building sites with fruit-trees, and laying down the orchards with grass. That enables the proprietor of the holding to enjoy the air space and freedom of the larger area without any appreciable outlay for maintenance, and it is more satisfactory and profitable to cultivate a small area really well than a larger one indifferently so.

It will be necessary to take a less price per acre for large plots than small, but the developer gains by getting rid of a bigger slice of his land. The principle of large gardens was pushed a little too far on part of this estate, and in one road four-acre plots were set out, but they did not sell. As a rule, purchasers of a building site seem to prefer not to have more than one acre; but after they have settled down they frequently find that they want more land, and the best plan is to set out plots with rather greater proportionate width than depth, as the latter can be adjusted by the sale of extra back-land in the future. An example of this habit of buying additional garden ground may be seen in the herbaceous road, described in Chapter V, as all the plots on the lower side were sold to owners of adjoining property in the rose road.

On the general subject of garden construction it is hoped the following suggestion will be forgiven —viz. that gardens should be laid out with more regard to the shape, size and aspect of the land and house, and also more in obedience to the principles of horticulture and to secure sunny sheltered spots in the winter and shade in summer, and less in compliance with the style of the day. It would cause more variety and individuality, and probably produce more lasting satisfaction, for gardening has become such a popular hobby that its modes rise and change very quickly.

Those who dress in what becomes them give and receive more pleasure than do those who follow fashion for fashion's sake. A buys the new kind of hat, which fortunately happens to be suitable. B has just bought a hat and suddenly realises that its popularity was already on the wane when it was purchased. B is unhappy till a hat has been obtained like A's, not because it suits A, but because it is quite the latest thing in headgear. C notices A's hat and admires it, but suffers no pain from the green-eyed monster, because C knows what is self-becoming and sticks to it. Pergolas, rock-gardens, water-gardens and herbaceous borders are each and all perfectly delightful in their proper places, but they are not all absolutely necessary, nor in some instances are they all desirable.

A little piece of water is often a great addition to a garden, and there are various methods of introducing it, from the formal pond or fountain in chiselled stone or moulded cement, to an attempt to represent nature as nearly as possible. One of the greatest difficulties in carrying out the latter is to hide the concrete edge of the basin satisfactorily when it protrudes above the surface of the water. By keeping the concrete well below the surrounding ground, and placing stiff clay all round above the cement rim, and then encouraging grass and waterside plants to grow over the clay, a fairly good effect may be obtained; but, after some experiments, the use of a material called tufa seems the best way of overcoming the difficulty.

Calcareous tufa is a deposit from running water, strongly impregnated with carbonate of lime; it is very like a stone sponge in some parts, and in others it resembles coral, or again a piece will be found like the *pimply* surface of a cauliflower. It is not affected by frost; seeds vegetate in it very freely; and under moist conditions it becomes moss-grown in a very short time. It is porous, so that its weight is light compared with its bulk, and if it is purchased in dry weather a ton provides much more material than the same weight of ordinary rock; but the greatest advantage which tufa possesses over ordinary stone is the ease with which it can be sawn assunder; it is thus not necessary to bury rather more than half of a spherical lump in the ground, as, when sawn in two, each half need only be buried 3 inches or 4 inches on the flat side in order to give the appearance of a portion of natural rock protruding through the soil. In pond-work it is most adaptable, as slices may be cemented on the face of the concrete structure which holds the water, giving the whole an appearance of nature without taking up much room, and the cement joints between the different pieces of tufa can be 'rough cast' with the same material pounded fine. It may be obtained from the neighbourhood of Matlock in Derbyshire. Probably no branch of gardening gives greater scope for the best or the worst taste in construction than rock-work. Some instances fascinate one immediately, and others, alas! look like a cross between the yard of a monumental mason and a giant nutmeg-grater. Tufa simplifies the work, because it is not formed in strata, and so there is no risk of committing the crime of placing the lumps at right angles to their apparent natural bed.

Pockets should be formed round the edge of a pond where it is desired to plant rushes, and if it is intended to stock with fish, sloping sides are better than perpendicular, as the former help to keep the cats from poaching. If water-weeds grow too freely fish are apt to lie on the top in a drowsy state and become an easy prey to pussy.

Though gold fish are usually chosen for stock, trout will live in quite a small pond, provided there are sufficient water-side and water plants and weeds to encourage the presence of insects. Brown trout do not grow much under these conditions, but the rainbow variety increase in size at a great rate if given artificial food; and their habits and movements are much more diverting to watch than those of the sedate gold carp. Four-inch fish will be fit to catch in twelve or eighteen months, and they take the fly ravenously. Rainbow trout have the reputation of being muddy flavoured, but if the water they are kept in is clear they are not at all bad to eat. The Surrey trout-farm supply fish at a moderate price, and if their instructions are complied with there is no risk in removal; but care must be taken in artificial ponds not to change the water all at once, for company's water, being sterilized, would kill them, if it were not allowed a week or so for exposure to the air first. Bread is bad for trout. King carp are interesting from the great rate at which they grow, and they will live in almost any water, but they should be the sole occupants of a pond, because most other fish eat their spawn.

If we except the wood-pigeon, the house-sparrow and one or two others, it is generally believed that birds, kept in due bounds, do more good than harm to horticulture, and the pleasure we derive from their habits and song leaves us their debtors. An increased interest in birds' nests may be created by hanging small boxes on the trees, about 4 feet from the ground, made with a small entrance hole, and provided with a lid that slides off or lifts up. Tits, wrens, robins and wry-necks are fond of building in these places, and if there are many birds in the neighbourhood most of the boxes will be tenanted for the nesting season. Robins are very erratic about their nests; sometimes they will desert if you touch a newly constructed home, but an instance has occurred here this year which showed a determined opposition to eviction. The coachman pulled down a truss of straw which stood on end in an empty loose-box, and in doing so a nest fell off the top. The man picked it up and stuffed it down on the floor behind a truss of hay; and the robins came and repaired the damage, laid their eggs, and are now bringing up their young ones.

During the war there must have been countless occasions showing the difference between nerve and courage, and one sometimes comes across them in natural history. There has been an example here during the past few weeks. A pair of

PLATE XI

missel-thrushes built their nest in the lowest fork of a tall silver birch, opposite the drawing-room garden door, and within ten yards of it, where there is frequent passing to and fro. The only conceivable reason the birds can have had for choosing such a public position must have been to be where they were less liable to theft from rooks and jays, but the hen was so nervous that every time a human being came near she darted off the nest at once; for the first week she would go if one only looked at her from the window. One Sunday a rook perched near the top of the tree. The old villain, who already had his white pouch full, must have spied eggs from aloft, as he at once began to crane his neck so as to see which was the easiest way down to the nest. But the storm-cock forgot all about its nervous fears, and rushed from its hiding-place full tilt at the great black thief and hounded him away, attacking him in the air again and again till he had flown out of sight. To-day the eggs must be hatched out. The parents for the first time changed guard. First the cock bird flew up and settled close by the nest, then the hen flew off, and the other bird hopped on its edge and spent some time in pounding a small worm to make it tender enough for such young digestions before stooping down and enticing one of the new-born nidicolous atoms to swallow it: they will not require much encouragement to open their mouths in a few days' time! When the hen came back to keep the young ones warm her fidgety care as to how she sat on them was very different from the casual way she used to sit on the eggs, though for the past two days she has certainly sat much closer than during any other part of the incubation. On looking later it was discovered that only one egg had hatched out, owing, no doubt, to the mother having been disturbed so frequently. Let us hope she is duly thankful that, as her child's family history has always been free from nidifugous taint, she will be spared for the present the anxiety attributed to the proverbial hen with one chick.

Reverting again to the subject of the war, it will be hardly necessary to point out that the absence of labour and the presence of patriotism have combined to render it more difficult to obtain good garden pictures just now. Plate II shows a lawn being cut with a farm mowing-machine, the result of which was $2\frac{1}{2}$ wagon-loads of hay; the second cut was made into ensilage. There is probably no greater saving in connection with the garden than leaving the lawns for fodder, for it does away with the hardest part of the work, the produce from which is of no practical value. On the other hand, if the crop is allowed to mature, it can either be made into hay or disposed of to some tradesman for his pony; and, as there must be thousands of acres of lawn in the country, it would be a great advantage if most of them were left uncut during the war. It is advisable to keep the verge mown, not only for the sake of neatness but to prevent the grass from seeding on the paths.

There is no horticultural expenditure of equal size which adds more to the appearance of an ordinary building than the provision of good climbers on the walls; and few things in the garden better repay the care bestowed on them than those which we train up our houses. Ivy and *Ampelopsis Veitchi* cling naturally to bricks and mortar, but most climbers require support to be specially provided for them; and the simplest plan is to drive nails into the joints of the brick-work as soon as it is erected, and then to stretch wire from nail to nail upright, horizontally, and crosswise. The building provides warmth, support and shelter to the plants trained against it, but it also possesses some disadvantages which must be remedied. In the first place the foundations protrude beyond the face of the walls, and the soil usually found round the concrete and brick footings is a mixture of rubbish and sour mould, and therefore it is necessary to dig out a rather large hole, and to fill it with good soil and rotten manure before the climbers are put in. Every gardener knows that wall-plants receive less rain than those in the open, but how few realise the necessity and the value of watering them, and tickling the surface of the soil soon afterwards. They will rise more rapidly if only a few main shoots are allowed to grow, and the rest are frequently pinched off.

One of the most rapid growers is the large-leaved Virginia Creeper, and it is not a bad plan to plant a few to cover some of the bare space while slower but more delightful flowering specimens, such as wistaria, are growing up. The last named requires much moisture, and for some years the young leaders should be tied in once a week during the growing season.

Conrad F. Meyer runs up a wall quickly to a certain height, and flowers early—the photograph on Plate XI was taken in May.

Climbing La France is a most admirable rose with larger flowers and fuller perfume than its shorter ancestor.

Clematis montana is a rapid grower and a free and early bloomer.

The design, workmanship and materials used in the construction of some houses are so good that it would be worse than useless to cover them with vegetation, but that class of building is exceptional: and most dwellings are so much improved by the growth of climbing plants that nearly every one admires a creeper-clad house, though strangely enough few take much trouble to decorate their homes in that way. Most people find it difficult to obtain all they want within the bounds they set on their expenditure, and so when they decide to build a house something has to be cut down in order to obtain the accommodation they require. Is it to be strength, sanitation, or beauty? In the revulsion against Victorian want of art, the tendency to-day is to go for architectural style—mainly a reproduction of the antique —at the expense of strength and occasionally also of sanitation; and it is here suggested that Garden First methods, including the planting of climbers, give a sufficiently attractive appearance to any building, which is decently proportioned and free from vulgarity, to set at liberty money that would otherwise be spent on architectural adornment.

Pray let it not be thought that this suggestion shows a lack of appreciation of good design. The charm of a well-planned elevation appeals to most people, and not least to those whose adjoining land is enhanced in value as a direct consequence. Moreover, the clever architect can often beautify up to a point without spending much extra money; but the fact remains that, as a rule, a good-looking building costs considerably more than a plain one of similar strength and containing equal accommodation.

Tennis lawns are often a trouble in landscape design, and on sloping ground it is difficult to make a court without interfering with the beauty of the garden, unless a formal terrace style is adopted. Where the gradient is only moderate, the angularity of the banks round the lawn can be overcome by accepting Hogarth's rule that the S curve is the line of beauty, and this has the additional advantage of lessening labour when the grass is cut.

PLATE XII

CHAPTER IV

ROADS

GOOD roads denote a high state of civilization; but, in the first chapter, so much stress was laid on the desirability of keeping a Garden First estate countrified, that some astonishment may be expressed on reading about the highly finished road recommended for some parts of a property developed on Garden First lines. It is a common error to look upon country roads as rough, muddy, and more or less neglected, whereas the truth is that they are in most cases just the reverse; for country people are fully alive to the advantages of good roads, and to the saving effected by keeping them in thorough repair: they know that directly the surface ceases to be waterproof dilapidation begins.

In the early stages of Garden First the roads, *quâ* roads, had no distinctive characteristics beyond the fact that they ran in curved lines instead of straight. The entire use of evergreen hedges, in place of walls or wood fences along the sides, gave them more the appearance of lanes than ordinary new streets, but the carriage-way and footpath were constructed in the usual manner. As the building sites on various parts of the estate came to be treated differently, it seemed that the roads also should vary. In one part, where it was intended to have four-acre sites, and the traffic was light, the paths were laid down with grass instead of gravel, and the paths round the village green were dealt with in the same way; whereas the roads through those portions, which were laid out at much greater expense, where considerable traffic was anticipated, have been finished with 12-inch by 8-inch granite kerb and a granite channel.

Taking the subject more in detail, a few words may now be said on the displacement of the straight roads, which are in general use, by those with curved direction. It is sometimes laid down as an axiom, that one road turning off from another should, when possible, do so at a right angle; but, surely, a gentle and gradual deviation from the direction of the predominant traffic is both better to look at and more convenient when driving, and so most of the Garden First roads have been set out in that way. It means the sacrifice of a certain amount of what is known as building frontage, and an additional cost for road-making; but the enhanced appearance of the place more than compensates for those drawbacks. It is hardly necessary to point out that though a curved way, leading naturally from one place to another, has an attractive aspect, nothing looks worse than a waggle without any meaning; neither can it be required to dwell on the importance of a correct tangential.

The following improved methods have latterly been adopted here in the manufacture of what are technically known as new streets. The usual custom on a building estate is to form and roughly metal the roads, with the idea that they will be properly 'made up' after the adjoining frontages have been completely built on. This method has serious disadvantages. It probably costs more in the end than it would to complete the road properly at first; the partly made carriage-way soon wears through, and puts a great strain on the horses carting materials on to the building sites; and it causes the occupiers of the earlier built houses to suffer much unnecessary discomfort.

One of the objections to making up a new road properly to start with is that the services, such as the telephone and the electric light, will cut up the surface and leave unsightly hollows or ridges where the mains and connections are subsequently put in. This may be overcome by a little foresight and arrangement. The sewers and water-main are, as a matter of course, laid while the road is being formed, and there is no reason why the other services should not be put in before the metal is spread; and not only should all the mains be laid but the connections should, at the same time, be taken across to each plot on either side of the right-of-way. Electric light and gas companies will agree to this method, when there is competition between them, but the latter do not love it, as they are afraid of leakages through settlements, though when the road is rightly constructed there is little risk on that score. They will also erect the lamp-posts on payment by the land-owner of a nominal rent till the lamps are lighted. The Post Office have met the matter most reasonably, and, on the understanding that the owner pays for making and filling the trenches, they not only refrain from erecting any poles on the estate, but put in the telephone main and connections underground to each road as it is formed. The only other probable disturbance of the road surface is for fire hydrants; but these can be put in by the freeholder, who will look to the local authority for the repayment of the cost when the hydrants become necessary for the public safety. There is much saving in this system as a whole, for there is less digging in making the various trenches than there would be after the metal had been put on, and none of the latter is lost in the process; and it must be cheaper for a supply company to do all its pipe-laying at once instead of in little bits. The great feature from a Garden First aspect is the comfort of having a good clean road from the first, with the knowledge that it will never be broken up.

It will be far cheaper for the developer to have the sewers laid by a contractor; but, to avoid the risk of settlement, the specification should include two punners to every filler, and this should be strictly enforced. Tunnelling should not be allowed unless working at a great depth, as it is impossible to fill up the cavity quite solid. If the sub-soil is chalk it pays to offer the navvies so much a yard for all the flints they throw out, and a little interest may be aroused by offering a prize for the largest unbroken stone.

It will probably be better not to have the metalling done by contract, and the following is the method adopted on this estate. At least 12 inches of chalk, after rolling with a 12-ton roller, forms the basis; then a layer of clinkers which goes down to about $1\frac{1}{2}$ inches after rolling; then two layers of dug flints, each 4 inches, and a final layer of hand-picked flints to the same thickness. Each stratum is tested every few yards by a wooden template cut to the camber of the cross-section required.

The proper curve from the granite channel to the crown of the road, and the correct rise from the curb to the back of the path, are subjects on which opinions differ. The steeper they are the cleaner will be the surface, but, if too steep the paths and sides of the carriage-way are not pleasant to use. The earlier paths here were found to be too flat; but in the later roads the cross-section is, if anything, too steep, and this is because, under the system of construction which has just been described, there is practically no subsequent settlement either through time or use.

The flints of the first two layers of metal are easily bound together with a little fine chalk, but the difficulty arises with the final coat. Chalk would, of course, be useless as a binding material owing to the action of rain and frost, and a common form of 'blindings' is the dirt swept from other roads; this certainly acts well in binding the flints together, but it always makes a dirty road—muddy in winter, and dusty in summer. An attempt was made to 'blind' the flints with clean, sharp sand, but it was unsuccessful; and then a mixture was tried of clean sand and clay. This answered the purpose very well indeed, but it took a long time to mix the clay and sand. Fortunately there happened to be a number of pockets in the chalk containing exactly the kind of material which was wanted all ready to hand—a sandy clay. These pockets are most curious; they are more or less circular in shape, and the sides are usually upright, perfectly smooth, and with a dark rind or skin. They supply excellent blindings, giving the road a perfectly clean surface; and no doubt this sandy clay could be bought should there be none on an estate.

The paths for these roads were founded with chalk, covered first with cinders, and then with about 6 inches of gravel, each rolled separately. In road-making, a great deal of material is often wasted through insufficient rolling, or imperfect levelling, of the previous stratum. It is difficult to keep all the paths on a Garden First estate smooth. Pedestrian traffic from one place to another helps to consolidate gravel, but the slow walk of those who examine what they are passing tends rather to rough-up the stones; and, in the dry weather which usually prevails when the flowers attract most visitors, it is not easy to keep the paths as smooth as they should be. It would probably pay to have a small motor-roller for them.

In roads of this description, great care must be taken that carts supplying building materials to the adjacent land do not carry away mould on the wheels or horses' feet, as that is sticky, and would cause the tyres of other vehicles to pick up flints. There is no risk otherwise, for the mud from other roads is short in texture and not sticky like poached mould or chalk; and it is worth a little trouble to have a carriage-way as clean as the footpaths. There is less labour in keeping a road perfectly clean than partly so, because on a clean surface it does not take long each day to pick up the droppings, whereas a dirty road has to be swept all over; moreover, in dry weather its unwholesome dust is being constantly inhaled. One of the difficulties in connection with this class of road is the motor traffic, and notices are put up restricting it to a low speed, with but partial success, because the temptation to scorch along a smooth, clean surface is hard for a motor-cyclist to resist.

To anyone starting a Garden First estate it would be an advantage to own a 12-ton steam-roller, or to share one with adjoining owners who may be developing their land. A 10-ton roller is not heavy enough for roads made on the specification described in this chapter, and a 15-ton roller is often, from its greater width, lighter per foot super than the 12-ton one. If a roller is hired, it is important to have it from a good firm, as the time wasted by an old engine and an inefficient driver far more than equals any saving in the rate paid per day for inferior work.

PLATE XIII

CHAPTER V

ROADSIDE DECORATION

LEAVING the construction of the road itself, we will now pass on to the decorative treatment of the land immediately on either side.

Before the war, the army was almost entirely drawn from the upper ten and the wage-earning population. This was sometimes thrown up against the middle classes, but the fault was not theirs; and the magnificent way in which they have lately responded to their Country's call shows that they are quite as patriotic as other ranks, but had previously lacked opportunity to prove it. Now there is another way in which workmen and the aristocracy have been in the habit of showing public spirit—viz. in the display by cottagers of their front gardens and window-plants, and by the systematic opening of their grounds to the public at fixed times, on the part of many large land-owners. That the majority of the intermediate classes have not so far given the public much sight of their flowers is more from the lack of opportunity and from force of habit than from any selfish inclination. The desire for privacy in one's garden is perfectly legitimate and natural, and so is the love of ownership; but the wish to possess objects of beauty without allowing others to see some of our possessions, when they could do so without disturbing our quietude or doing damage to our property, would be bad. The system of floral roads carried out under Garden First methods overcomes this difficulty to a very large extent. Flower-beds are formed on either side of the road, but protected from the public by a slight wire fence. These flower-beds are set out to be viewed as a whole decorative scheme by those using the footpaths or carriage-way, but they are divided as to ownership amongst the several frontagers according to the width of the holding they purchase. The privacy of the remainder of each building site is preserved by a hedge running at the back of the flower border; or further seclusion, if desired, may be gained by planting plenty of shrubs.

Thousands of people come to see the blossoms during their seasons, and the residents have shown, by their ready acquiescence in the arrangement, how glad they are to be able to afford others so much harmless enjoyment. The scheme of decoration may not always be exactly what each owner would have chosen, but he merges his own ideas in thought for the general well-being; and as a medium voice, which is of little use for a solo, may be an excellent member of a chorus, so one section of the flower-bed acquires its full value as part of the whole border.

Floral decoration of the roadside is capable of endless variety, but it was perhaps natural to choose the Queen of Flowers for the first experiment in that direction, and the notion that roses would lend themselves well to that style of treatment has not been dispelled by subsequent experience. The site of the new roadway was for the most part through pasture, some of which was very fibrous. For about half the length the top soil rested on chalk, and for the remainder there was about 1 foot of clay between those two strata. The first step was to deep-plough both the site of the 40-foot road and a strip on each side of it measuring 20 feet wide. The whole of the top soil was then removed from the road surface on to the two 20-feet strips. Of these, a width of 6 feet 6 inches, next to and on each side of the road, was intended for a turf path, and therefore the poorer soil was used for that purpose and the better quality retained for the two 13 feet 6 inches rose-beds beyond. In order to stiffen the soil in the portion where there was no clay, as much of that substance as was found on the site of the further half of the road was brought to the first part and incorporated with the light mould when the beds were being formed.

In carrying out the foregoing and similar Garden First work, two contrivances are very desirable. The first is a giant plough, which is much stronger and capable of ploughing much deeper than an ordinary one. Some idea may be formed of the amount of earth it turns over in making these roadside borders, or in cultivating previous to the planting of belts of trees, when it is mentioned that as many as eight heavy cart-horses have been used on it at one time. The plough stands this strain well, but the chains frequently break, and spare links, whippens, etc., should be handy. It is rather fascinating to watch, as when ploughing into the chalk it sings a sharp note; or, if it is going through deep ground previously well cultivated for a flower border, the ridge of earth falls over like a little brown wave.

The other invention is a light railway with skips, or small steel trucks, that can be tipped over when unloading. The use of these rails saves a great deal of horse labour, as the wagons run downhill alone, save for a man on the brake; and it obviates cutting the ground up, as carts would at once do in any but dry weather, which on a Garden First estate is important.

An illustration of the plough appears on Plate I. The ploughman beside it has worked on this land for twenty-nine years; he has given up his team, and his age entitled him to a pension twelve months ago; but though he was one of a family of thirteen, with a total income of 13*s.* per week without cottage, he still rises with the lark, and is not likely to retire from active work for many a day. The Garden First light railway cannot be photographed, as it was given to the Ministry of Munitions; and the trucks, which were stamped with a German name, are now employed in what will prevent the future dumping in this country of goods made in Germany.

But to return to what may be now called the rose road; the beds having been well cultivated by the big plough and thoroughly manured, the next thing to do was to plant the roses. And here a mistake was made in ordering the whole 6,000 odd to come at one time, as the work of sorting and labelling that number of prickly bushes in the cold wind and rain on short November days was unpleasant. There were 400 varieties. The tall climbers were planted 5 feet 6 inches apart at the back, then a row of half climbers and tall bushes, then a row of moderately strong bushes, and then in front and nearest the road a row of small dwarfs and pom-poms. The climbing roses were returned across the border at each boundary of a plot, and slender rustic poles were placed perpendicularly and horizontally for their support.

Finally, they were all labelled in a manner legible from the public footpath.

Great care was taken with the planting; some friable soil had been kept dry under cover to fill in with, and three men were employed to plant each rose—one to dig, one to hold the bush, and another to spread the rootlets. If one man is employed to hold the rose-tree with one hand and spread the roots with the other, he is apt to forget the latter duty; but if a man is told off specially for the purpose of placing the roots correctly, he realises the importance of his work and performs it conscientiously. The results exceeded expectation, and the following summer one could pick a couple of large laundry baskets full of exhibition blooms, and then feel uncertain that the best had not been left behind. This is not the place to discuss rose culture in detail, and there are numerous books on the subject, though probably none surpass the Rev. A. Foster-Melliar's work, which has been recently co-edited by the Rev. Page Roberts and Mr. Herbert E. Molyneux. It is full of the information a grower should possess, is entirely devoid of padding and perfectly easy to understand, so that by it a beginner can win prizes during his first season.

A very important question in these floral roads is that of fencing: something that will enable the passer-by to see the flowers, without making it easy for any evil-disposed person to steal them. In America they seem to be able to do without fences to their front gardens; and in Portland, Oregon, U.S.A., there are said to be 2,000,000 Caroline Testout roses along the streets; still in this country we do not seem quite ready for such complete trust. It was prophesied, when the rose road was first started, that it would not answer because so many blooms would be stolen; but, as far as is known, not a single flower was improperly taken before the whole of the land changed hands. The fence employed was a galvanised wire-netting one, 4 feet 6 inches high, $1\frac{1}{2}$-inch mesh, 16 gauge. This was attached to strand wires with steel standards 1 inch by 1 inch by $\frac{3}{16}$ inch angle-iron, and these latter were painted an inconspicuous green. This sort of boundary is really much more difficult to surmount than a wooden fence or brick wall, as it is not very rigid, and there is also the risk of torn clothes through the short pieces of wire that bind the netting to the top strand. The standards should have plates riveted on below the ground level to make them firm enough, and, wherever the road curves to any extent, they will require side-stays to prevent the straining of the strand wire pulling them over. The holes in the standards should not be larger than is necessary for the wire or they become a source of weakness.

A detriment to this kind of fence is discovered when it is cut in two to make an entrance on to the building site, and care must be taken to provide new strainers before the wire-netting is pulled out of shape. It is desirable to lay the turf path 4 inches back from the wire fence, otherwise the grass grows up through the netting, when it is difficult to deal with and seeds on the public gravel-path.

Partly in order to gain more security, and partly for effect, gates are placed at the entrances to these roads, and this fact, coupled with the presence of a lodge or cottage adjoining, has perhaps a restraining influence; at any rate no crowd could possibly be more sedate and orderly than is to be seen walking along the rose road on Saturdays and Sundays during July. The gates at the entrance to the rose road are shown on Plate XIII, and they and the other iron-work illustrated were wrought by hand at the village smithy. There appears to be no regulation to prohibit a local authority taking over roads, the entrance to which is guarded by gates, should they wish to do so; and, provided there is some apparent reason for those erections beyond the supposition of mere exclusiveness, it does not seem in bad taste to have them. The simple oak gates at the exit from the rose road, and shown on Plate XIII, were considered more in harmony with the less formal surroundings than wrought-iron would have been

PLATE XIV

at that point, as it is there where the rose road joins the lane with grass paths already referred to.

In describing the different roads, their real names are omitted, and it will answer the purpose to refer to the next one as the bulb road. The actual names were chosen for their appropriateness and to be in harmony with Garden First ideas, without having recourse to recent styles whose popularity is likely to be their downfall. The bulb road winds along the level summit of a hill towards the village from a steep approach which leads up to it through a little piece of forest. No description is given of that original woodland height because it needed no Garden First treatment except a care to disturb it as little as possible; but it may be of interest to record the size of one of the trees, an old silver birch, which measures 8 feet 6 inches round the base 1 foot above ground.

The entrance gates to the bulb road are shown on Plate XII, the lodge on Plate XIV. On either side of this road are four rows of silver birch-trees carpeted beneath with grass, in which live many sorts of bulbs and wild flowers, with a few naturalised tame ones. In order that the trees should grow tall and graceful and not become shrubby and too overhanging, they were planted somewhat near together, and have twice been thinned out, with a certain amount of 'siding up' of the remainder. In carrying out the latter operation on birch-trees it should be done only in the winter as they bleed badly when the sap is flowing. For the same reason it was decided to do the thinning out in the spring, as it was impossible to dig up the trees to be removed without destroying many bulbs and plants, and if birch-trees are cut down and not killed the roots are very apt to shoot up again. In buying small silver birches from a nursery it is advisable to have some stiff stakes inserted in each bundle, otherwise the slender leaders are very liable to be broken off while the trees are being transferred to the railway truck.

The season on this road starts directly after Christmas, with the snowdrops and aconites, and goes on to crocuses, daffs, primroses, violets, snakesheads, cowslips, anemones and tulips. Most of these things do exceedingly well under the half-shelter from frost and sun afforded by the silver birch, and few people will deny that the flowers enumerated are much enhanced in beauty by a green grass setting. In fact, some may even say with regard to daffodils that they soon become monotonous and are easily overdone on arable ground. It is most important to see that the grass-seed for this purpose contains only the shortest growing varieties and not a grain of Pacey, as it is impossible to cut the grass while the flowers are out or the bulbs are coming up, and rank herbage drawn up by the trees in spring is most prejudicial to the whole scheme. Through a lack

PLATE XV

of care in this respect the present road was much hampered during its first season, for the grass grew 3 feet high and had to be cut with pocket-knives to save the bulbs, at a cost of about £40.

Perhaps the weakest part of this particular design is the incompleteness of shield between the far side of the trees and the remainder of the building sites. In the first place a single row of tall privet was planted to form something of a hedge, but it did not quite harmonise with the effect desired, and was removed, leaving the question of privacy to promiscuous shrubs and individual taste. Probably most residents would consider ability to see the spring flowers from their house of more importance than absolute seclusion, for one seems to take more interest in, and derive greater refreshment from, what blooms early in the year than the more luscious blossoms that come later. The far end of this road leads on to the village green, and, there being no gates at that spot, the direction was given a double crank as a slight check to the speed of motors.

The next attempt at roadside decoration took the form of a herbaceous border along one side of a road which leads out of the rose one. Though this way also is somewhat curved for its whole length, it runs mainly East and West, and as it is on a slope facing North it seemed a good opportunity to fill up the adjacent ground on the lower side with mould, and then form a flower border facing southwards to the public road. In this instance the whole of the soil from the surface of paths and carriage-way was used to make the one bed, so that it had an average depth of nearly 4 feet.

In the two floral roads previously described it was found that, although the wire fence could be seen through, it still slightly interfered with the enjoyment of the flowers by the public. So this time it was decided to have a low wire-netting fence 3 feet 3 inches high in order that passers-by might look over the top with ease, and yet tall enough not to be mistaken for a seat. Security was provided by making a ditch on the far side of the fence and building a wall below the wire up to the level of the public footpath, so as to form a kind of haw-haw. The bottom and other side of the ditch were grassed, as well as a level strip, 5 feet wide, to form the private path in connection with the border, and the flower-bed itself was 12 feet wide.

In order to form a background for the herbaceous plants, both as shelter against cold winds and for appearance, and in order also to give perfect seclusion to the low-lying land beyond, a good privet hedge was planted on the North side of the border. As the ground was heavily manured and would be highly cultivated, it was important to prevent the roots of the privet hedge from stealing what was intended for the herbaceous plants, and to obviate this a slate wall was sunk parallel to and on the South side of the hedge. This wall was composed of slates measuring 2 feet by 1 foot, set upright so that their tops were 4 inches below the surface of the soil, and the joints were overlapped 1 inch and cemented. The hedge was encouraged to keep its roots near the surface, and, so far, they do not appear to have trespassed on the flower border.

It is unnecessary to give a detailed description of the plants used, but the idea was to increase the length of season occupied by herbaceous plants proper, and with that object bulbs were freely used to make an early beginning, and some dahlias and chrysanthemums postponed its end. Again, a border nearly one-third of a mile long with nothing but herbaceous plants would be rather monotonous, and to avoid this the side boundaries of the adjoining building sites were projected across the flower-bed by a double row of half-climbing roses; a few tall umbrella roses were added here and there, and also some topiary specimens in box, which appear to give more enjoyment to juvenile visitors than the children derive from all the rest of the show. No attempt was made at a graduated colour scheme, partly because of the length of the flower-bed, but still more because the various sections would be eventually owned by different frontagers, who would be unlikely to continue the original combinations in their entirety. The entrance gates shown on Plate II are not finished, and wait for the termination of the war for their completion. The granite pillars are 12 feet 6 inches high and 11 feet round the base, and these gates are the largest on the estate, as they had to do duty for two roads curving away from them on the side from which the photograph was taken.

The available space for floral roads is now almost used up, but one has been started for the display of various kinds of flowering trees and shrubs of which there are such a great variety. In setting out this road some uncertainty was felt as to the best way to deal with a rather large kidney-shaped clump of Scotch firs and Austrian and Weymouth pines, of about forty years growth, in order to preserve the trees as far as possible. It was decided that if they were included in two or three plots of land they would inevitably be cut down by the purchasers in order to use the space they occupy for houses and gardens, and that the better plan would be to drive the new road right through the middle. This meant the sacrifice of a portion of the interior trees but the saving of nearly all the outer ones, so that as a unit in the view the clump would not be spoilt. This treatment also had the advantage of leading the public through the deep shade of the pine wood to bring them out into the bright contrast of the flowering trees beyond. Or, coming in the opposite direction, the firs make a capital background, which is rather a want, as so many flowering trees bloom before their leaves are out.

The scheme was started five years ago, and some of the leading nurserymen were asked to send boxes of cut blooms of all their best flowering trees and shrubs from time to time. This they kindly did, which enabled one to make a list of the best and most attractive specimens, so far as they were not unsuitable to the position and soil the trees were intended to occupy. In the following season a sufficient number of trees were purchased and placed in a nursery on the estate to try for a short time how they would answer at a higher altitude; and the majority of them have since been planted out along sides of the new road. Most of them appear quite hardy and to like their quarters, and as some pains were taken over their selection their names are given below. It will be noticed that several foliage trees are included, for some of them are quite as beautiful as the flowering varieties; for instance, *Catalpa bignonioides aurea* is as brilliant of leaf as the flowers of laburnum, and avoids the unsightly after-crop of seeds which that tree is troubled with. Moreover, the golden foliage of the one lasts far longer

G

than the racemes of the other. Some of them are extremely beautiful, and *Amygdalus Davidii alba*, the white almond, which is a mass of bloom in a mild January, is a most useful addition to any garden. If picked in bud every flower will come out perfectly indoors, and it will last a fortnight.

A hedge of common sweet-briar was chosen as a screen on the land side of the two belts of flowering trees. In the nursery it was surprising to see how nearly all the colours harmonised, but now they are planted out one can see a few that will need re-arrangement: for instance, some of the peaches are a difficult pink, and look very unhappy near a ribes.

List of Trees and Shrubs for the New Flowering Tree Road at Garden First.

Name of Tree.	Variety.	Name of Tree.	Variety.
Acer	colchicum rubrum	Berberis	fascicularis
	macrostachyum (passiflorum)		ilicifolia
			Knightii
	Reitenbachii		stenophylla
	Schwedleri		Thunbergii
Aesculus	alba fl. pl.		vulgaris atropurpurea
	Briotii		
	Pavia rubra	Buddleia	variabilis magnifica
Amelanchier	canadensis	,,	Veitchii
Amygdalus	amara	Calycanthus	floridus
	Davidii alba	Caryopteris	Mastacanthus
	,, rubra	Catalpa	bignonioides aurea
	macrocarpa	Ceanothus	thyrsiflorus
	Persica alba	Cerasus	J. H. Veitch
	,, magnifica		multiplex
	,, rosea		serrulata
	,, rubra		Watereri
Berberis	Aquifolium	Choisya	ternata
	Darwinii	Cistus	florentinus

ROADSIDE DECORATION

Name of Tree.	Variety.
Cistus	lusitanicus
Corchorus or Kerria	Japonica
	,, variegata
Cornus	elegantissima aurea
	Kousa
Coronilla	Emerus
Cotoneaster	buxifolia
	Simonsii (bush)
	,, (standard)
Crataegus	Carrierii
	double scarlet
	,, white
	pendula
	prunifolia
Cydonia	alba grandiflora
	Japonica (red)
	,, coccinea
	,, Moerloesii
	,, nivalis
	,, Simonsii
	Knapp Hill Scarlet
	Maulei
	,, alba
	Millardii
	umbellicata
Cytisus	albus
	capitatus
	nigricans
	pallidus
	purpureus incarnatus
	scoparius andreanus
	,, praecox
	virgatus
	Yel. Broom scoparius
Deutzia	candidissima
	discolor major
	Lemoinei
	Wellsii
Diplopappus	chrysophyllus
Escallonia	exoniensis
	Langleyensis
	macrantha
	,, Ingramii
	montana
	Philippiana
	rubra

Name of Tree.	Variety.
Fagus	purpurea
Forsythia	suspensa (Fortunei)
Genista	daurica
	Hispanica
Hamamelis	arborea
	mollis
Laburnum	Adamii
	aureum
	vulgare
	Watererii
Lonicera	albiflora
	involucrata (Ledebourii)
	Standishii
	Xylosteum
Negundo	albo-variegatum
	aureo-marginatum
	Californicum aureum
Philadelphus	Bouquet Blanc
	Conquête
	Manteau d'Hermine
	purpureus maculatus
	Rosace
Prunus	Padus single
	Pissardii (bush)
	,, (standard)
	sinensis, alba fl. pl.
	,, rosea fl. pl.
	spinosa fl. pl.
	triloba
Pyrus	Aria chrysophylla
	coronaria
	,, fl. pl.
	floribunda
	,, atro-sanguinea
	Malus Neidzwetzkyana
	Scheideckeri
	spectabilis
Raphiolepis	japonica
Rhodotypos	Kerrioides
Rhus	Cotinus
	glabra
Ribes	Gordonianum
	missouriense

Name of Tree.	Variety.	Name of Tree.	Variety.
Ribes	sanguineum	Syringa	Madame Kreuter
	,, glutinosum		Madame Lemoine
Robinia	Bessoniana		Marie Legraye
	Decaisneana		Michael Buchner
	hispida		President Carnot
	inermis		President Grévy
	Neo-Mexicana		sibirica
	Rosynskiana		Souvenir de Louis Späth
	viscosa		
Rubus	deliciosus		Wm. Robinson
Spiraea	alpina	Tamarix	caspica
	amurensis		hispida aestivalis
	Anthony Waterer		indica
	callosa		tetrandra
	,, splendens	Ulex	Double Gorse
	,, superba	Viburnum	Laurustinus
	Douglasii		Opulus sterile
	formosa		plicatum
	nobleana	Weigela	amabilis
	pachystachya		
Staphylea	pinnata		,, alba
Stephanandra	flexuosa		Bouquet de Fleur
Syringa	Charles Joly		Cameleon
	La Tour d'Auvergne		candida
			Conquet
	Leon Simon		Eva Rathke
	Madame Casimir Perier		rosea
			Van Houttei.

PLATE XVI

CHAPTER VI

HOUSES

IN the opinion of the occupier a garden is a more or less necessary adjunct of the house. From a Garden First point of view the house is but the complement of the garden in a general survey of the estate. The latter conclusion will have considerable weight in deciding on the style of house to be built or allowed in the earlier stages of development, when the use of main-road frontages and the nearness of the station indicate the desirability of erecting smaller residences than will be required later.

Two detached houses, on frontages of 75 feet each, appear more crowded than one pair of semi-detached houses on a plot having a frontage of 150 feet. It will, therefore, best carry out Garden First principles to begin by setting out the land for houses in pairs; and a recent alteration in some local authorities' bye-laws, doing away with the necessity of protruding an ugly party-wall above the roof of two attached buildings, removes what was the one great disfigurement to semi-detached houses when considered pictorially. Back additions are quite unnecessary where ground is plentiful; and, provided they are tabooed, and equality of treatment in the design of the back and sides with the front is granted, the Garden First effect of semi-detached houses is equal to, if not better than, that of detached ones. The rooms are greater in number and smaller in cubical contents than in a detached house of equal size to the pair, so that a quainter and more cottage-like appearance can be obtained. The greatest detriment that the occupier experiences is the noise of his semi-detached neighbour, and it can be almost shut out by a 14-inch party-wall.

It is clear, however, that, if semi-detached houses are decided on, it will be necessary for the vendor of the land to build them; for an intending resident cannot erect one semi-detached house by itself, and he would not wish to be troubled with the building of the other house of a pair and the uncertainty of letting or selling it afterwards. It may in certain cases be possible to sell the land to builders, but they are not as a rule willing to start a new and untried neighbourhood; neither, till they have had some experience of it, are they likely to appreciate or respond to Garden First methods. Recourse may be had to 'financing,' but besides the well-known objections to that system, it would not tend to make a good start in the opening up of a Garden First neighbourhood.

As to detached houses, it will probably be found that, except on very restricted lines, they cannot be built by the land developer and sold at a sufficient price to realise the cost of building plus the figure at which the land should sell by itself. This is mainly due to the smaller number of applicants for larger properties and to the greater independence of the wealthier man, who naturally prefers to put his own ideas into practice with the help of an architect. If, therefore, the owner of an estate is forced to build detached houses other than those he desires to keep for investment or those which he wishes to erect as examples, it implies that he has failed in some way to make his land sufficiently attractive.

In undertaking building operations the land developer has the choice of two methods. He may engage a foreman builder to buy the materials and engage and superintend the labour, or he can have the houses built by contract. Provided he can find the right man, the first method has certain advantages—viz. ease in making alterations, the avoidance of 'extras,' and greater facilities for garden construction in conjunction with the building operations. On the other hand, the latter plan will probably turn out the more economical. Satisfactory contracts for building may often be made informally by a private arrangement when both parties are known to each other; but should it be decided to place the work out to tender, it will be necessary, or at any rate advisable, to obtain professional assistance; for in view of the fact that the interests of the contracting parties run mainly in opposite directions—a point which is emphasised from the start by the acceptance of the lowest tender—it is wise to have an independent architect or surveyor to see fair play on both sides. There is also the question of detailed specifications and bills of quantities; and, even in the event of the developer possessing the requisite technical knowledge, he will probably find it unsatisfactory to add that work to his other occupations more directly connected with the Garden First side of development.

In tackling the subject of building it is necessary to remember that the main point is not so much the sale of the houses themselves, as the effect they will have on the remainder of the estate and in creating a building market for what has hitherto been farm land.

While disclaiming any desire or right to advise on the various arts and crafts which are touched on—his knowledge of those matters being often at best but a discovery of his own mistakes—beyond their direct application to and influence on Garden First development, the writer is bold enough to call attention to the illustrations on Plate XVI. This semi-detached house was designed after some experiments in trying to arrive at the greatest amount of internal comfort with the minimum of domestic labour, and also at what was in harmony with Garden First ideals in inexpensive outward appearance. The plan, made in 1895, has been used repeatedly on the Garden First Estate, and has been more or less copied in hundreds of instances elsewhere, but its imitators probably formed an exaggerated idea of its value through not making sufficient allowance for its original garden setting. The low roof plate, while necessary to obtain the effect desired, has the drawback of lessening the tie which the joists of a level ceiling would afford, and of decreasing ventilation when that is not obtained from side windows at a greater height. In order to remedy the latter to a certain extent, little outlet ventilators were placed over the doors and just under the ceiling to take the used-up air away to the loft.

More than one chimney corner is illustrated, for, notwithstanding the fact that the old 'down fire' is but a relic of bygone times, an inglenook fitted with a modern stove adds much to the enjoyment of a hall or living-room: it provides seats for two people, who may have come in feeling very cold, where they can quickly obtain a warm glow all through; it sends out a more genial and less scorching heat than a stove fixed in the side of a room; and it prevents two or three people planting themselves immediately in front of the fire to the exclusion of everyone else from its influence.

It is customary, in framing restrictions for a building estate, to stipulate for houses of not less value than a given sum in any particular road, and it seems difficult to do away with such a custom. It has, however, rather a snobby flavour, and the notion that A objects to live next to B because his neighbour's house is not quite so large is most unpleasant. So in building houses it has been the custom here to place a detached house now and again between semi-detached ones of half the size; and one never hears the smallest objection raised by those able to rent or purchase the larger building, and the varying size of the structures tends to prevent monotony. Again, the custom has been adopted of building a lodge or cottage at the entrance to the floral roads; and so far from being looked on as undesirable neighbours, these lodges have appeared to act as an attraction in helping the sale of the plots immediately adjoining; and the unusual sight is seen of a cottage let at 5*s.* per week in juxtaposition to a house that must have cost some thousands of pounds to erect.

PLATE XVII

HOUSES

It is not very easy to design a nice-looking two-storey detached cottage without running to some extra expense for decoration or construction; and the reason is that, although the area of ground which it covers is so small, the height of the rooms under the ordinary bye-laws must not be less than those required for a large house, and the cottage so arranged looks like a match-box set on its side. The upper photo (taken in winter) on Plate I is an illustration of it. This cottage was put up hurriedly along with the farm buildings, which at that time were quite away from roads or houses, and it has to thank the rapid growth of trees and creepers for any modification of its plainness. Another two-storey detached cottage, which is shown on Plate XVII is somewhat similar in shape to the one just referred to, but more pains were taken with it. The appearance of height is reduced by hanging-tiles on the upper part of the walls; and the use of antique roof-tiles and iron casements helps it to take full advantage of its Garden First setting.

Local authorities seem to be considering a revision of their bye-laws with respect to workmen's houses; and if those as to height of rooms were reduced in the case of detached cottages in open situations, it would enable much better-looking places to be designed, and the tenant would enjoy more floor space without increased cost; and if some effective form of compulsory ventilation were discovered, there could be no conceivable disadvantage.

In Garden First architecture and garden planning some skill and care are necessary, if it be desired to represent the antique, in order that the general newness of the completed work may not be too apparent. Old bricks and tiles and roof stone quarried long since are often very beautiful if procured from country districts, but they are difficult and expensive to obtain, and one may succeed in treating new material in such a way as at least to take the raw edge off its crudity. For instance, stone, bricks, and tiles laid out separately in long grass on the north side of a wood soon become weathered and moss-grown, and oak quickly mellows in the same way.

CHAPTER VII

FINANCE AND LAW

ALTHOUGH it would be presumption to attempt to advise generally on such a speculative purchase as land for building development, a few comments on certain financial aspects of Garden First schemes may not be out of place. One point, which must not be lost sight of, is the compound interest to be allowed for, not only on the cost of the land, but on the larger cost of development plus the expenses of management and upkeep of the unsold portion from time to time. In order that this shall not swamp the profit, it is not advisable to pay more than about £150 per acre for the whole estate—being land which, while not far from a station, is at the time of purchase only agricultural.

A reasonable distance from a railway that offers a short ride to London or some other city is of the first importance. Conveniences in the shape of domestic supply will not be slow to meet the demand created by a new district, and such means of transit as the motor-'bus or tram will probably follow all too quickly for the real welfare of a neighbourhood largely dependent on sentiment for its success and popularity. It requires some courage to talk of sentiment when discussing the financial and legal aspects of building development, as the word is easily confused with sentimentality; and, like love and lust, praise and flattery, these words—in their essence the antithesis and not the complement of each other—have a similarity sufficiently true to make it difficult to know where one ends and the other begins. Still, the fact remains that sentiment plays a very important part in Garden First work; and it would probably be better to subsidise a quiet-looking horse brake to and from the station than allow the ordinary type of London 'bus to take its place. Motor-'buses and trams are often of great use to the working classes; but, in those districts where the wage-earner is dependent on his wealthier neighbour for work and wages, it is a doubtful kindness to the workman to provide what may seriously interfere with the local labour market, though in other respects it may have been to his advantage to have the cheap rides.

On the question of title, the advantages of registration under the Acts of 1875 and 1897 are obvious, and, if the land is not already on the register, it is advisable to have it entered at once; and it is worth while to stipulate in the contract for the purchase of an estate for this to be done, so that in the event of the original title not being sufficiently clear to pass the Land Registry, the agreement to buy may not be binding. Having once registered the title it is bound to satisfy all sub-purchasers who apply for portions of the estate, as it is indefeasible. The original registration entails some expense, and buyers of plots may not save a great deal if they pay a solicitor as well as the registration fees, but the costs to the land developer when retailing are small. One great advantage is the ease with which transfers of registered land may be read compared with the old-fashioned conveyance. The former is a sheet of foolscap in clear type, with a few blanks filled in with legible writing; and, as the printed form is always the same, only the written part need be carefully read. The old style of conveyance, with long lines of writing difficult to read, had to be gone through with a finger or thumb on each end of the line to mark the place; and it was necessary to read the whole with much care, each conveyance being probably drawn by a different lawyer. One was never quite sure, even after the unregistered title had been passed by solicitors to many different purchasers, that the next lawyer would not discover some minute flaw which would cause much worry and expense to remove. The plans the registry supply are excellent, being always clear and accurate, and their surveyors the very best; but a word of warning may be given on the subject of restrictions entered on the register, as, once there, it is very difficult to obtain an alteration, even at the desire of both parties to the arrangement.

The present seems a good opportunity to discuss restrictive covenants, and the following have been found satisfactory as a basis of Garden First sales:

Stipulations.

1. No building shall be erected on the piece of land hereby agreed to be sold or any part thereof other than one detached house and stabling domestic offices and greenhouses and other outbuildings appurtenant to such house. Such house shall not cost less than £   the cost to be reckoned for material and labour of construction only and not to include any stables or outbuildings. Such house stabling and outbuildings shall be erected in accordance with drawings and elevations previously approved by the Vendor.

2. No house erected on the land shall be used for any purpose other than that of a private residence. No house shall be designed for or occupied as flats nor shall any trade business profession (school) or manufacture be carried on on the said piece of land. Nor shall anything be done thereon or by the Purchaser's user of the road known as   that shall become a nuisance or annoyance to the adjoining owners.

3. No part of the land shall be used as a public road or as a means of access to other property.

4. No boundary or party fences or party walls shall be erected on the land other than wire fences and live hedges and the Purchaser shall do all that is necessary to maintain such parts of the live hedges as are on his ground.

FINANCE AND LAW

5. No building shall be erected within   feet of the road and no house stabling coach or motor house within   feet of the side (or back) boundaries.

6. The Purchaser shall pay a fair proportion of the cost of maintaining the road known as   until it be taken over by the Local Authority and shall not cause any excavation to be made in the road without first paying a fine of £3 to the Vendor for permission to do so.

7. No traction engine or heavy motor propelled vehicle shall be used for drawing building materials or minerals on to or from the said land.

8. The hedges at the back and two sides are party fences and the Purchaser shall bear his fair proportion of maintaining the same.

9. No chalk gravel or sand is to be taken out of the said land other than as much as may be necessary for ordinary building operations and for the purpose of laying out the garden.

10. The Purchaser shall see that a proper roadway on to the land is made with old sleepers or otherwise before the building materials are brought on to the ground or chalk or earth removed therefrom.

11. No clothes except children's garments shall be hung out to dry unless hidden by a hedge or other suitable enclosure.

12. The Purchaser shall maintain the plantation (flower border) in front of the said land as part of a general scheme but this is not to prevent a reasonable amount of thinning out or openings on to the said land.

Clause No. 12, for maintenance of the front border or plantation, will, of course, vary with the different roads. It is desirable to have some restriction of the kind, though, except in rare instances, it would no doubt be found sufficient to trust to the *esprit de corps* of the various owners.

There are two special covenants which it has been found desirable to include in leases and tenancy agreements on a Garden First estate: first, against keeping bees, which, like dogs and cats, seem very different if they belong to other people; and the apiarist may fondle his pets unharmed, but the neighbours whose flowers provide the honey are regarded by the armed insects as undesirable aliens during the shining hours. A hive of bees was once brought here and placed in a lavender field to experiment on the honey so obtained. For some reason or none, all the bees seemed to go mad; and they stung everybody they could, and even the horses, so that the work on the estate had to be stopped till nightfall, when the hive was removed. The second covenant is against the use of a lawn mower within nine inches of a tree stem, as the nut on the side of the machine is certain to tear the bark off unless the mower is kept right away from the trunk.

While we are discussing legal matters, a word may be said on the question of road widening, which is very apt to crop up when one is turning farm land into building ground. It is now settled that the widening of an old highway repairable by the public constitutes the right of way a new street, within the meaning of the Public Health Acts. As this enables the local authority to make up the road with kerb, channel and paved paths at the expense of those owning the adjoining land, it is desirable to consider whether the road or lane is suitable for such treatment, before any widening or removal of the old boundary is carried out. A local authority's contract to take over the strip dedicated to the public by the landowner is not binding on the council till it receives their seal, and one must recollect that bodies of men will sometimes do corporately in the name of the community acts they would scorn to do for themselves individually. Moreover, the modern idea of good government is the greatest good for the greatest number, or, in other words, the benefit of the class which is numerically strongest, and so it is thought righteous for the many to tyrannise over the few and for the people to disregard the claims of the individual. This is a distinct advance on the good of the few at the expense of the multitude, but the highest form of government can only be attained when all men are treated with equal fairness.

Disputes between land developers and local authorities are usually settled by reference to the Local Government Board. When the inquiries are private it is an inexpensive method, avoiding the horrors of a law-suit, and, on the whole, the results are probably equitable as between the ratepayers and the individual. One cannot, however, get over the fact that the Local Government Board, while acting in a judicial capacity, have a policy to pursue; and that there are times when the appellant may be prejudiced in his case through an error committed by the board while acting in their executive capacity. In such circumstances a certiorari in the High Court may be applied for, but few would care to face the worry and expense such an appeal would involve. There is also, in special cases, a reference to Parliament; for instance, an adjoining local authority recently tried, at the suggestion of the Local Government Board, to forcibly absorb the district of which the Garden First Estate forms part. The adjoining Council had ruled their own neighbourhood on up-to-date London lines, which, however good for their own people, would have been unsuited to a district whose prosperity is largely dependent on the development of Garden First principles. The neighbouring authority gained its case before the Local Government Board, but lost it again in the House of Commons on the second reading.

Although it is desired to induce others to take up the kind of work which is here described, it is impossible to avoid a reference to the Finance (1909–10) Act, 1910, as it has had a marked effect on land development; and, so far as it has decreased confidence in the stability of real property as an investment, it will tend to prevent such undertakings as Garden First more than other schemes for the disposal of land, which are not likely to

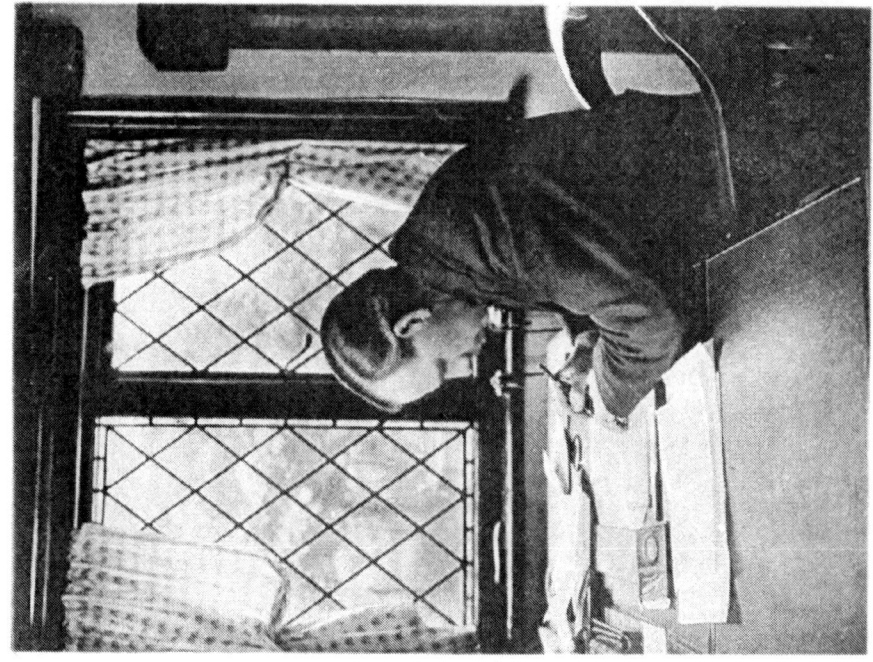

PLATE XVIII

take so long to work out. It is most unfortunate that such an important industry should be made the subject of party politics; and in the following comments the endeavour will be to keep the remarks as party colourless as possible.

It is unnecessary here to decide whether it is ethically right or wrong to charge an increment tax on land and not on other forms of investment; it is enough that it has been decided to do so by the majority of electors. There is also no doubt a general feeling amongst all sections of the public that if an individual makes a large profit out of land, which has gone up in value in consequence of other men's expenditure of brains, labour and capital, while he himself has done nothing, that the owner should pay to the people some share of his profit, unless they have been receiving in the meantime some advantage through the space being kept clear of buildings at a loss of interest to the proprietor. A tax of this kind would rarely, if ever, impose any burden on a land developer; and, if he had the right to claim for decrement on his ground being injured by popular action, he would probably be a considerable gainer on the whole, provided the onus of proof on both sides rested with the claimant.

Unfortunately, the existing Act does not work on the foregoing lines. In the first place, it is so difficult to understand that the task of complying with the law, and particularly that which relates to the valuations required at the present time, seems to be almost hopeless; and the worrying work necessary to carry out the 'Land clauses' in connection with an estate in course of development is, to those who have not experienced it, well-nigh incredible.

Then the owner pays on his profits without allowance for his losses; and his power to obtain exemption from the impositions is more dependent than it should be on his cleverness and experience.

The undeveloped tax is so assessed that a premium is offered for small gardens instead of large, and for the construction of premature and unnecessary roads that depreciate by effluxion of time and lock up capital, against tree planting, which increases its own value and that of the surroundings as the years go by. The argument that an undeveloped tax is necessary to prevent 'holding up' cannot be applied to a man whose business is to sell his land; for the experienced developer is aware that there is no greater sin against his own interests than that of stopping sales by asking more than a fair market price for his ground. His stock-in-trade is so valuable in proportion to the annual turnover, that loss of interest on his capital is his greatest financial difficulty; for though his stock will not depreciate by keeping, in the way that a milliner's does, it will not appreciate in the way that a wine merchant's is supposed to do.

Again, if A. and B., two small owners, are equally engaged in the development of a new neighbourhood, increment duty would be charged A. on that part of the increased value of his land attributable to B.'s expenditure, and B. would be liable for taxation on that part of the increase in value of his land due to expenditure by A. On the other hand, if C., a large landowner, is engaged single-handed in developing the whole neighbourhood, he has the right to escape duty altogether. But the worst of it is that A. and B. are not only penalised by law for their small stature, but each has the Herculean task of proving what portion of the increased value of his property is not due to his neighbour's expenditure but to his own.

Again, the landowner who sticks to his ground and declines to sell, experiences comparatively little trouble through the Act, as the occasions when it operates rarely occur; and it is the trouble and work and worry and loss of business which mainly affect those who are actively engaged in selling in still smaller pieces their little fragment of the world's surface, far more than the taxes. In fact the owner of this property was informed on the highest authority at the time the Bill was passed that he would never have to pay 1s. increment duty on the whole of the

Garden First Estate. He will probably also pay little or no undeveloped tax; but the satisfaction of relief from taxation at the present time is to most men small indeed, compared with their regret at the loss of every sovereign profit out of which they could pay 5s. towards the war. As a revenue producer an undeveloped tax concurrently with increment duty must be a failure; for, to such an extent as the former forces sales by increasing the vendor's desire to sell without promoting the purchaser's willingness to buy, land will be prevented from rising in value to the detriment of increment duty.

The crux of the whole matter is this—viz. whether private or State ownership of land is the better. If the latter, the Finance Act makes a good start in that direction. There is as usual something to be said on both sides. The private ownership of land, with its responsibilities and opportunities, gives an artificial, or, at any rate, an exaggerated appearance of wealth to the possessor, and is for that reason more apt to cause jealousy than forms of investment that are not so obvious. In agricultural districts those landlords are often most envied who derive least profit from their estates by reason of their generous expenditure. It is probable, however, that most men do not wish for State ownership, and it is certain that they would not approve of syndicalist methods to attain it; and, if the writer's views are correct, the trouble is bound to find its own remedy before long. The Act has so far done good service in helping to arrest the decay of unpopular neighbourhoods and to let off basement dwellings; but no one wants a house famine, and, if rents go on rising, the public will take the matter into their own hands, and so adjust the laws of the country as to prevent them interfering with the building trade.

If it is true that all wealth comes from the land and that the primary needs of man are food and shelter, it is bad policy to harass either of the classes that are causing the earth to produce the two chief necessaries of life, or to treat it on less favourable terms than classes with occupations of minor importance to the people. A shortage of food pictures unadulterated poverty, but the small house often carries with it a touch of romance; and so the corn ground was mostly let off, and the building land left to take its chance with the Finance Act. In most instances the disputes of honest men on religion and politics are due to their not understanding one another; and if a Royal Commission were held to inquire into the land clauses of the Finance Act, and all parties, including those with practical experience, were invited to give evidence, it would disperse a vast amount of misconception and ill-will, and just and useful legislation would be insisted on by the electors.

Large profits are sometimes made out of land with very little trouble, and that knowledge no doubt helped to pass the Bill, under a vague idea that these profits proved an automatic rise in the value of ground. That is, of course, incorrect: they are due to the fact that, there being no certain market for real property, the prices vary widely, and, partly by good fortune, and partly by knowledge and foresight, a purchaser may, from time to time, buy an estate which will show a wide margin on resale, at the expense, nine times out of ten, of the late vendor. It is hazardous trading for a big profit, and it is doubtful whether the average speculations in land show a higher rate than the risk warrants. At all events, it is an open market, and certainly not an over-crowded one at the present time.

The reported objects of the Land Clauses of the Finance Act were to obtain revenue from unearned increment in respect of land and to prevent the latter being 'held up.' The law referred to is clearly useless for either of these purposes and should be repealed; but there is no reason why any necessary legislation should not be passed to enable a duly constituted authority to force owners of land to sell when it is clear they are selfishly hanging on to their property to the detriment of the public welfare. And with regard to obtaining revenue from accretions of capital, the present hard times for the Chancellor of the

Exchequer offer an excellent opportunity to tax increments of all kinds. Securities are very low in value at present; and, if the State received a proportion, say 20 per cent. of the increase in price that stocks and shares, as well as land and houses, realised in future beyond their total cost to the vendor, the yield would be enormous, and the tax would be paid by those who are comparatively well off at a time and under conditions when they would least feel the disbursement. It would not affect those who had suffered financially because their investments had gone down in value owing to the war, but only those who are buying now or who will shortly be buying in a rising market and selling again at a higher price. Stock jobbers and land developers could receive differential treatment, as they already pay a tax on their profits. The machinery would be comparatively simple and the scheme would not interfere with thrift like a direct tax on capital; and it would have this additional advantage, that it would afford an opportunity of decently burying that part of the Finance Act, 1909-10 (1910), of which even many of its original supporters would be glad to see the last.

Another piece of legislation in recent years, the Town Planning Act, should, on the other hand, be of service to those contemplating Garden First work. Opinions vary considerably as to the fairness of this law, but though it is said by those who have tried it that the trouble of carrying out a town planning scheme under the Act is great, the ideas the latter contains seem excellent. It saves the owner who is developing on good lines from running the risk of a serious injury to his undertaking through the inferior methods the owner of an adjoining and unrestricted estate may adopt, and it prevents the latter from taking advantage of the market created by his neighbour to that man's detriment. It gives confidence to the purchasing public, inasmuch as they know that the amenities of the neighbourhood will be respected. Any parliamentary legislation which is prejudicial to land development must in the long run be borne by the people; but injury to a particular neighbourhood by a local authority or proprietor will be borne by those owning property in that district and by the tradesmen who have been carrying on their business there.

Talking of owners, the advantage which accrues to any place from the fact that the residents are freeholders and not tenants is enormous, as the whole population have the same interests to guard and a comparatively equal stake in their maintenance. Empty houses will rarely be seen, as an occupying owner is unlikely to leave till he has sold his holding to an intending resident.

One of the first decisions to make, on the purchase

of an estate, is what use the land shall be put to pending its being sold or built on. Much, of course, will depend on the quality of the soil and the purpose to which it has hitherto been applied, and recent events will influence one's decision both on the score of patriotism and on account of better prices of produce. Apart from the foregoing considerations, it will probably answer best to lay down the whole to grass as soon as it is clean enough, for that gives it a more Garden First appearance. It is true that the hedges and trees to be planted will prevent stock being turned out to graze, except when the enclosures are large enough to warrant the expense of fencing. Still, the additional labour of cultivating a number of small areas compared with one large field must be thought of, and, if not very closely watched, a deficit will soon appear on the farm account, as building estates are not usually chosen for the richness of their soil. The grass will probably pay for cutting, and if there are any plots near a neighbourhood without proper gardens, application should be made to the Vacant Lands Cultivation Society, who are doing excellent work in utilising vacant or derelict pieces of ground.

On the question of labour, it may be pointed out that it becomes slightly complicated by the employment of several different classes and types of men on one place, such as farm hands, estate labourers or gardeners, builders' men, and navvies, each with different views of life, customs, and wages.

Perhaps the following experiment may be interesting, as a small contribution towards the wages question. Some years ago it was decided, on investigation, that those estate workmen who did not live on the place were not receiving quite enough for a man and his family to live on, and it was arranged to give them a small increase; but it was felt that the bachelors did not really need more than they already received, though their work was worth just as much as that of the men who were married. A device was hit on to get over the difficulty, and it answered very well indeed. Neither class of men received any extra cash each week, but it was credited them on a card, on the understanding that the married ones could draw out whenever they had a little extra expense to meet, but that bachelors could only receive theirs once a year, for the purpose of taking a week's holiday during which at least half of the bonus was to be spent in railway fares. There was a little difficulty at starting in popularising the idea. One man, after saving up for twelve months, said he never had had a holiday and he didn't want one. However, after the first experience, it was voted a great success, and it has been no small pleasure when hundreds of miles from home to run up against one of the workers with whom one had been in close contact, as master and man, for the past year.

It is a misfortune that there is no distinction made between the income of the married and the unmarried workman, for, while the former has a difficulty in making two ends meet, the latter has in normal times only to pay about twelve shillings per week for his board and lodging, plus insurance and clubs, and the rest of his wages are for his clothes and pocket-money. Most lads are brought up as teetotallers, and a larger proportion would remain so, were they not tempted to break their old habits by the sudden rise in their income, without corresponding liabilities, on attaining a man's strength. Besides, their ideas soon grow to their means, and then any thought of marriage is checked by the knowledge that practically all the personal pleasures they have become accustomed to must be given up. They could afford to pay more insurance money during bachelordom with very little feeling of loss, and, if the money were saved for them against their marriage or old age, they and the State would reap the full benefit of it.

There are incidences of income taxation that particularly affect land developers, and they are due in the main to the long period that a whole transaction in estate disposal takes to complete and to the difficulty of valuing stock in hand for which there is no market. Different methods of assessment are adopted by Surveyors of Taxes, who have the power to alter and re-alter them at their discretion with a retrospective effect for from three to six years that even Laban did not insist on. At first sight this seems less than just, but before condemning the Surveyor of Taxes one should state one's case to one's business friends, and one would find that each of them had a tale to tell of the treatment he had received under schedule D which was at least as sad as the sufferings one had borne oneself. One then realises that one is not by any means alone, but that all men are treated equally unfairly, and so the unfairness does not really exist. The comfort the taxpayer derives in this way is both psychical and mathematical, for he knows that he has not been singled out for particularly harsh treatment, which the consciousness of having occupied a useful place in the work and trade of the nation would make it hard to bear, and he also realises that if everyone received from the Surveyor of Taxes the treatment that in his own opinion was fair, the rate per £ would have to be considerably increased in order to obtain the national revenue, and so he would be no better off in the end.

The two principal systems for assessment of land development profits are:—

A. To credit the account with purchase moneys received and debit it with the *pro rata* prime cost of the land sold, plus the whole of the expenses of development to date that are not in the form of buildings, it being considered that the latter have a saleable value, but that the cost of roads, tree planting, and the like can only be turned into cash as the land is disposed of. This method generally involves what amounts to the bringing forward of a balance of expenditure during the early part of a development.

B. To credit the account with the sales for the year, and debit it with the *pro rata* prime cost of the area sold during that period, together with a proportionate share, according to the acreage sold, of the expenses of development incurred during the same twelve months. This arrangement presumes the rest of the estate to be increased in value to the extent of the remaining outlay.

It is desirable that there should be a fixed system of income-tax accounts in regard to land development, and also some clearer division between what property may be sold as an investment, without any payment of income-tax, and what investments are liable to that charge when sold beyond their cost.

On Plate XIX may be seen a small dairy herd, and as one of the most pressing social questions is that of the milk supply, a few words on that subject may, perhaps, be forgiven.

There are at present certain bye-laws regarding the cleanliness, infection, purity, and quality of milk for the protection of the public, and no doubt dairymen as a class carry out these regulations thoroughly, but the system is faulty. The minimum standard of fat is only three per cent., and it would not be practical to put it higher, but, as artificial colouring matter is allowed, there is not sufficient inducement to go beyond the proportion of fat required by law. The consequence is that nearly all milkmen keep cows, such as shorthorns and British Holsteins, that will produce a large quantity of poor milk, with the prospect of a good sale to the butcher directly the lacteal stream does not pay for the board and lodging of the beast.

There is also the vexed question of bovine tubercle, which is only illegal in dairy stock that are so affected in the udder or are in an advanced stage of consumption. It is reckoned that about one-third of the cows in this country are affected with tuberculosis, and experiments with milk show that there is often a larger percentage of bacilli in nursery milk than in ordinary samples. It is difficult for the lay mind to understand why science has so far failed to decide definitely whether tubercle in cows is communicable to man, but the common feeling

PLATE XIX

FINANCE AND LAW

of parents is distinctly opposed to feeding children on milk produced by animals suffering from that disease.

Now, in order to obtain a high standard quality of milk some other method must be adopted than exacting a legal minimum, and in order to eradicate consumption from cattle without ruinous expense for compensation, some different plan must be devised than an order for the slaughter of infected beasts. One solution of these difficulties would seem to be to empower and encourage Local Authorities to provide and maintain dairy farms, as the importance of the end to be gained and the difficulty of gaining it in any other way would probably more than balance the drawbacks inseparable from municipal trading.

Only Channel Island cows should be kept by the Council when the conditions are favourable, and the Guernsey is the hardier and more useful of the two varieties. It looks well in winter, when the Jersey is a sorry object to behold, and it is practically as rich in cream as the latter. The Guernsey, though not considered in England a dual purpose cow, will supply yellow beef fairly quickly when she ceases to be profitable as a milk producer. She will thrive on land where a shorthorn would do badly, and the former gives at least as much milk as the latter in proportion to the food they respectively eat.

Only cows that pass the tuberculin test would be kept by the Local Authorities, and only sound bulls from sound dams would be used. No colouring matter or preservatives would be allowed. The object would be to produce the best article, and not the cheapest, and thus not crush private enterprise but afford a high standard to compete against. Any scheme to enable the poor to buy the municipal milk would be a national question, and should be kept clear of the accounts of the Council's Farm Committee.

Perhaps some disappointment may be felt if this chapter is closed without more definite information or advice on the profit to be derived from developing land on Garden First lines, compared with what may be made by the disposal of it in the ordinary way. It would be exceedingly difficult to reply accurately to a question of that kind. The net price realised per acre by Garden First treatment would probably compare unfavourably with that realised by the sale of the same area through ordinary methods. On the other hand, the latter will only prove effectual in disposing of a very limited amount of ground close to the railway station; and, when that land is gone, no demand will arise for the rest of the estate, which will remain farm land till increasing population forces a slow growth outwards on ordinary suburban lines. There is, how-

PLATE XX

ever, another side of the question, which it is hoped this little book will help to illustrate, and that is the satisfaction to be derived from a Garden First employment if it can be engaged in without too much financial anxiety; and to many who will have gone through the great war an outdoor life will offer considerable attraction.

CHAPTER VIII

THE VILLAGE

FIFTEEN years ago a village was started in the far corner of the estate, the cottages of which were to be occupied by men working on the place. A green of nearly four acres was laid out in the centre, encircled by a road, on the other side of which now stand a score of cottages and houses, which are well screened from public gaze by a thorn hedge, trees, and tall shrubs.

Somehow or other, the workmen did not care to occupy the cottages, which were offered them at a rental within their means; and, at one time, it looked as though the houses would be empty. On the other hand, the place has since become popular with people of good social position, and artists, authors, city men, members of Parliament, and musicians have taken up their residence there. In fact, so popular did this village become, that it was found necessary to take steps to prevent it turning into a colony of week-enders. One gentleman from

PLATE XXI

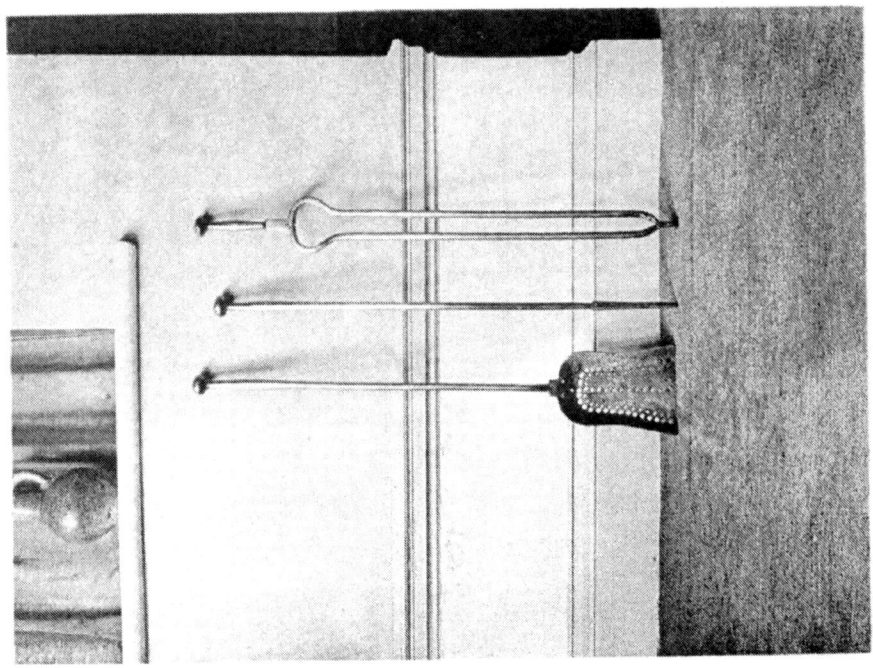

PLATE XXII

town who expressed his determination to lead the thimple life (*sic*), and, to that end, was anxious to rent one of the cottages, merely stipulated for the addition of a billiard room, and that the little window in the chimney corner should be fitted with a casement to facilitate the supply of whiskies and soda on to the tennis lawn.

But to return to the description of the village: the houses are mostly built of brick, and, as a rule, the lower part is roughcast. Few substances keep out the rain in an exposed position so well as good roughcast, applied first as a coat of cement and sand, next as a coat of cement, lime, and sand, and, thirdly, shingle mixed with cement and water. The lime is added to the second coat to make the shingle adhere better. The stones composing the shingle are, of course, absolutely impervious to water, so that there must be less evaporation going on on the surface of the wall than in the case of bricks or porous stone, and therefore the house is warmer through the winter months. Then, again, the liquid cement, forming part of the roughcast, has a tendency to gravitate downwards while it is drying, which makes a number of small 'drips' that must tend to guide rain drops away from, and not towards, the wall.

The smithy is roofed with stone, and three other buildings with old tiles; but the remaining cottages are all roofed with machine-made tiles, and certainly lose something in appearance for that reason; at the time they were constructed, nice-looking hand-made tiles with nibs were not so easy to obtain as they are now. The gardens vary in size from thirty-six poles to nearly two acres. The Village Inn supplies teas to visitors, and is also the post-office and general shop; the coffee-room, with its sanded floor, has a chimney corner and a bow window glazed with crown glass.

The lower part of the house shown on Plate XXIII is built of red sandstone with Portland stone quoins; and the iron casements for this and many others were wrought at the village smithy. A forge is a great acquisition on any Garden First estate, though it is not every smith who is good both at horse-shoeing and at some approach to Art smithing. As well as gates, there are many iron fittings, such as strap hinges for doors, which are much more satisfactory if home made, and there is frequently some repairing to be done to machines and implements. On Plate XXII are some home-made fire-irons and a very strong oak and iron harrow. The latter is useful for loosening the surface of a road after all the top soil has been removed, when the heavy flints would prevent even a strong plough being used; it can be further weighted by a heavy slab of stone.

The chestnut tree, which spreads its branches to

PLATE XXIII

prevent the heat of the forge being increased by the summer sun, had not been moved for more than twenty-five years, when it was transplanted to the village. In order to give it a fair chance to recover from the shock, the roots were pruned to within about three feet of the trunk six months before it was shifted, and the trench round was refilled with good compost. This method was not altogether satisfactory; it certainly induced a large quantity of fibre to grow in the trench in thick masses about two feet long; but it seems as though the better plan would have been to ram the trench tight with poor soil, and then to do everything possible to induce the formation of new fibre within the ball itself instead of in the trench. However, the tree has not done badly, and warranted the cost of its removal, which took eighteen men and some strong horses to accomplish.

The stocks and whipping-post were made on the estate within the last fourteen years, but one of the London weekly illustrated papers has since given a photograph of them with the following descriptive paragraph:—

Relics of Old-time Punishment.

The Famous Whipping-post and Stocks at . . .

In a few English villages may be seen, even at the present day, interesting relics of bygone days, which often puzzle those who see them to account for their former use.

The pretty little village of . . . possesses two such curious relics of the olden times. These are the whipping-post and stocks, and, as will be seen from our illustration, they are joined together.

It was the custom in bygone years for the authorities of . . . to put people in the stocks for various offences, and those guilty of serious crimes were tied to the post and whipped. Happily, these degrading forms of punishment are now things of the past.

A see-saw, on one side of the green, is well patronised by young people in summer; a few seats are provided for the weary; and the public are allowed as much access to the open space as is compatible with private ownership and the welfare of the residents. Football and hockey are played there, but the ground is not level enough for cricket, which is hardly a disadvantage, as the latter game would be dangerous with so many children about.

Geese were kept on the green for some years till dogs made the place unsafe for them; and, although they are quaint creatures, they had their drawbacks, and their departure was not generally regretted. Beyond planting willows on the south side of the pond, nothing has been done to make it either beautiful or in harmony with an old village scheme, for it was designed solely that boys might sail their toy boats there. A path runs round it between the water and the fence; and the latter, being a few inches higher than the depth of the former, prevents children

PLATE XXIV

using the pond who are too small to climb out should they have the misfortune to tumble in.

Of the slight adverse criticism which has been aimed at this portion of the estate, the main part has been directed towards the absence of hard drinks at the inn. Though some distance from the station, there is no part of the property where houses are now so much sought after; and opinions from various sources warrant the hope that the village possesses, in some degree, the restful quality that was aimed at in its formation.

In the chapters describing Garden First, the endeavour has been to rely mainly on personal experience. Still, it does not follow that much of what has been said is not already well known; but those details are, for the most part, included because they have been found of essential value in Garden First work and are emphasised accordingly.

There is a word which has been avoided in the foregoing pages as it is one not to be lightly used; it is the word 'charm,' and the author is conscious of a deficiency of that indefinable and delectable quality at Garden First. He is, however, firmly convinced that if the system which has been outlined is carried out by abler hands, by men trained in art and possessing a fine knowledge of horticulture, who, not being mere copyists, are imbued with the spirit of the antique and who know and love nature, it is feasible to make new neighbourhoods having charm as one of their chief attributes, and that there are possibilities for the creation of the beautiful in the garden development of building land as truly as in the use of marble or canvas.

Printed by SPOTTISWOODE, BALLANTYNE & Co. LTD,
Colchester, London & Eton, England

Lightning Source UK Ltd.
Milton Keynes UK
UKOW021900111212

203531UK00006B/393/P